The Small Business Owner's Guide To Protecting Your Business From Hackers

CHRIS WISER

The Small Business Owner's Guide To Protecting Your Business From Hackers

Published by Prominence Publishing, www.prominencepublishing.com

The Small Business Owner's Guide To Protecting Your Business From Hackers-- 1st ed.

ISBN: 978-1-990830-11-2

Contents

Foreword

By Chris Wiser

As cybercrime continues to rise at an alarming rate, it is now more important than ever to ensure that your business networks are protected from hackers, your employees are properly trained to recognize cyber-security threats that could wreak havoc on your business, and that businesses are implementing a strong cybersecurity plan that will help mitigate the threat of cybercrime. Cybercrime threatens all businesses across the world; regardless of size or revenue, the likelihood of being hacked is imminent. Unfortunately, it is not IF but WHEN your business will be hacked.

What are you doing to protect your business from the evolving threat of cybercrime? As cybercriminals continue to evolve their tactics, business owners will need to increase security measures to not only safeguard their financial assets, but also their business data, from being stolen or compromised. Too many times we hear of business owners turning their cheek to implementing cybersecurity measures to then have their business completely devastated by a cyber-attack. How much can you afford to lose in terms of both time and money? Remember, you must ask yourself this question as a business owner when it comes to protecting your business from cybercriminals.

Protecting your business from cyber threats is crucial to your ongoing success and should be your top priority as a business owner. Most business owners are familiar with the term cybersecurity but do not completely understand the need for it in their business. Cybersecurity is not a commodity; rather it is a necessity for every business owner. Understanding your cybersecurity risks and vulnerabilities is important in protecting your business assets and data from cybercriminals. Cybersecurity experts have created strong methods to mitigate cyberattacks and threats to your business. Protecting your business assets is crucial to longevity and continued business success.

In this book, we have brought together 13 cybersecurity experts to help business owners protect their businesses from cybercriminals.

Chris Wiser, CEO, 7 Figure MSP

Speaker/Trainer/ Entrepreneur/ Coach

5 Reasons Entrepreneurs Need to be Aware of Cybercrime

By Mike Skinner

Every business is an opportunity for hackers to steal data, but many entrepreneurs think that they can't possibly be a target since they are usually small businesses with fewer records than large enterprises. In fact, small businesses are more frequent targets than large enterprises, because hackers know that small businesses do not have the advanced infrastructure and cybersecurity staff to stop even the least sophisticated attacks. Small businesses are often easy targets, but they don't need to be.

Every year, Verizon releases the Data Breach Investigations Report[1], which is a great resource for anyone to review the latest trends in cybercrime. The top issues that continue to trend as popular vectors for hackers are phishing, ransomware, and credential theft. These three issues are likely to cause a data breach in a small entrepreneurial business that falls victim to cyber-threats. Even the smallest data breach can be the end of a startup or small business, making it critical that founders find ways to stop cyber-threats.

Cyber-Attacks and Breaches are Costly and Can Kill a Startup

The number of attacks grew sharply during the pandemic, mainly because an at-home workforce lacked cybersecurity controls typical in an in-office staff environment. Even though corporations are pushing more workers to return to the office, the threats haven't reduced in number. In 2021, organizations saw an average of 900 attacks every week. This means that every business faced128 attacks every day, and businesses either stopped them or became the next victim.

Data breaches targeting large corporations cost them millions, but much of the monetary loss is from litigation, a loss in customer loyalty, and brand damage that can last for years. As an example, Target suffered from one of the largest data breaches to date in 2013. They finally settled a class action lawsuit in 2017 for $18.5 million, but the total estimated loss for Target is over $200 million in litigation and sales losses.

For a small business, just a few hundred thousand in lost capital can mean bankruptcy. Downtime from an attack costs businesses thousands every hour. You might think that your small business won't lose as much, but small businesses often don't have the resources to quickly recover from data loss, leaving them vulnerable to long-term downtime and negative revenue impact.

Ransomware, one of the most common threats, can cripple business productivity for weeks. The attack often starts with a phishing email. Phishing attempts can be mitigated using email filters, but many startups avoid spending too much on cybersecurity measures because they think it is unnecessary. Email security is one of those cybersecurity strategies startups skip as a future "like to have" and not a "must have." With just one successful target, an attacker can install ransomware on the startup environment and rapidly encrypt and lock critical files.

Once ransomware installs on the environment, it scans the network for shared folders and files and encrypts them with an irreversible cryptographically secure algorithm. It's impossible to decrypt files unless security researchers find ways to bypass the ransomware author's scheme, and most ransomware is resistant to bypasses. The only way to recover is to use data backups, but many startups have poor disaster recovery strategies including no backup schedules.

Several small businesses have closed due to ransomware attacks. The Heritage Company in the UK, Travelex in the UK, and a US-based healthcare provider Wood Ranch Medical have all closed due to losses from ransomware attacks. The National Cybersecurity Alliance polled over 1,000 small businesses and found that a severe data breach put 10% out of business.

Your Reputation Rests on Your Ability to Protect User Data

In the post-Snowden era, people are much more interested in the ways businesses use their data. In 2018, the Facebook Cambridge Analytica scandal exposed Facebook disclosing about 87 million of their users' data. Cambridge Analytica used Facebook user data to interfere with important political campaigns and country voting interests. The outrage made even more headlines and convinced more people to be concerned about the way their data is being used.

The aftermath of data misuse and leak scandals led to several compliance regulations enacting laws around the way corporations handle consumer information. The EU's General Data Protection Regulation (GDPR) and The California Consumer Privacy Act (CCPA) were both created after Facebook's misappropriation of user data, and several more are in the pipeline.

Facebook's scandal cost them $5 billion in Federal Trade Commission violations, but the long-lasting effect is that many users lost trust in the organization. For a startup, the impact on revenue, brand damage, and the loss of customer loyalty can bankrupt them. Startups have enough competition from larger businesses, so news of a data breach can tip the scales in favor of competitors and negatively affect investor interest.

Reputation and transparency about the way a startup handles private data will support customer trust. Brand trust is a strong driving force in sales and revenue, and trust lies in several factors including data privacy and protection. Just one critical mistake could mean that customers will ask for their data to be removed and find another business to work with.

Small Businesses are a Bigger Target Due to a Lack of Cybersecurity Resources

Hacking is a business, and your startup's data is worth money. Depending on the data that you store, user data can be worth[2] up to almost $250 per record on dark web markets for qualified financial data. Data used in a data breach can give attackers access to online banks and transfer services where attackers can earn almost $1,000 per qualified record. Once a financial impact on a consumer leads back to your small business, it could mean hefty fines related to compliance violations and extensive litigation costs.

Before you think that you don't have enough records to attract attackers, your startup could be one of several targets to collect small portions that will be part of a large dataset. Hackers will target several small busi-nesses to build a long list of records to sell on dark web markets. A small business might only have 500 records, but stealing these records will add to the other dozens of small businesses with a few hundred records. With enough qualified data, a small business can be a part of a seven-figure payout for an attacker.

As an entrepreneur, you put a larger target on your back if you don't have a cybersecurity plan. The owner of a startup is an even bigger target. CEO fraud and spear-phishing target executives specifically for their elevated access privileges. In a small business, there are few executives (sometimes only the owner), and attackers know that these users have access to most (if not all) network resources and data. Their elevated privileges make them a target for attackers who know that most small businesses do not have the cybersecurity defenses or training to prevent phishing.

Credential theft is also common and starts with a phishing attack. Hackers use phishing emails to send users an embedded link that points to a web page that looks like the corporate site or a common productivity resource (e.g., Gmail or Office 365 documents). The malicious web page displays a request for a user to authenticate. If the targeted user does not notice that the page is on a malicious domain, the attacker can often trick the user into entering their credentials. Once the attacker has a user's credentials, the user's network is open to unauthorized access and a data breach.

In addition to a data breach and without proper cyber-security monitoring, your business could have an un-authorized user present on the network for months before detection. In fact, IBM reported[3] that the average time to detect a threat on a network is 256 days, and the average time to contain it is 82 days. That means many organizations take almost a year to deal with a threat, giving an attacker plenty of time to steal data, trade secrets, intellectual property, email messages, and other important information on users and your small business.

A lack of cybersecurity resources to prevent, defend, and identify attacks can lead to reputational damage. When customers hear about your lack of security or how long a threat existed on your network, it hurts your reputation and ability to attract customers.

Cybercrime is Hard to Detect, Even After You've Been Already Been Hacked

To add salt to the wound, many small businesses think they've removed a threat from their environment, but advanced persistent threats (APTs) use methods to bypass removal from a system and avoid detection from future monitoring efforts. APTs are in a class of their own, as they grab a foothold on network resources, become very difficult to detect, and often leave back-doors that give access to the network even after it has supposedly been contained.

An APT moves laterally, which means that it exploits other vulnerabilities on the network without any detec-tion. APTs can spread rapidly and exploit thousands of machines and vulnerable network equipment. One example is the WannaCry ransomware, which Microsoft determined to be launched by an online cyber-criminal group named Lazarus Group.

The Lazarus Group has been tied to several infamous attacks such as the Sony data breach in 2014, the Bangladesh bank heist in 2016, cryptocurrency and pharmaceutical attacks, and the most famous WannaCry in 2017.

WannaCry took advantage of a vulnerability in the Windows operating system, so any person simply on the internet with a Windows computer would be vulnerable. The malware was installed on hundreds of thousands of computers without detection, and it remains an issue to this day. Several more destructive APTs exist on the internet, and they take advantage of small businesses that don't have the resources to fully detect, eradicate, and monitor for future attacks.

Having fewer cybersecurity resources makes it much easier for attackers to exploit vulnerabilities because large enterprises have the monitoring capabilities and security teams to make it harder on attackers. Even with enterprise-level cybersecurity infrastructure, some of the largest tech companies with the best cyber-security experts on staff have been the victim of data breaches. Amazon, Apple, and Facebook have all suffered from data loss after a breach.

Humans are the Weakest Link

It's common for startups to build good relationships with employees, and employees often become trusted members of the workplace. Long-term employees might have unfettered access to data, and the startup trusts that the employee won't do anything nefarious.

Insider threats are one of the biggest security risks for any organization, especially small businesses. Not every employee is a malicious risk. Some employees are at risk of simply being a good target for phishing and malware. Regardless of the reason, humans are the biggest risk to your small business, and insider threats are the most difficult to detect since they have legitimate authorized access to most data.

The two most harmful attacks using insiders are social engineering and phishing. Both can lead to additional exploits such as malware, ransomware, credential theft, and botnet activity. In most cases, the attack begins with a phishing email targeting several employees or a specific one known for high privileges. An attacker might perform reconnaissance by researching LinkedIn for corporate organization structure, email addresses for high-privileged users, and names of employees. With this information, the phishing campaign begins.

In enterprise business, email security stops phishing emails from reaching the intended recipient. Email security is commonly missing in a small business environment, which means your data's security is left to human intuition. An employee must know the signs of a phishing email to stop an attack, but it only takes one employee to fall for phishing for an attack to be successful. The risk of human error is something all corporations strive to reduce.

Small businesses usually have no content filtering capabilities, so employees have unfettered access to the internet. This too, poses a security risk, as drive-by downloads are also vectors used to trick employees into installing malicious software. Without the right security in place, users could install rootkits and remote-control software giving a threat actor full control of the local machine and access to the network and its stored data using the targeted employee's account.

Numerous data breaches start with a simple email message, but another common attack uses social engineering and phishing to steal money from small businesses. CEO fraud occurs when an attacker hacks a high-privileged user's email account or sends fraudulent email messages that look like legitimate senders. The latter is called spoofing, and it's common in phishing emails. Attackers will register similarly spelled domain names as your small business to trick users into thinking the message is from an executive or the business owner.

As an example, Google and Facebook have fallen victim to email fraud where attackers were able to steal $100 million using fraudulent invoices sent via email. Large technology companies have plenty of training to help users identify phishing and fraud, but even the most highly trained employees can fall for well-crafted social engineering and email-based attacks. It's why no company will ever be able to completely eliminate cybersecurity risks, especially when there is reliance on human action to stop attacks.

A Few Tips to Help Stop Common Threats

Entrepreneurs have a lot on their plate to create a successful startup, and cybercriminals threaten their success. Although cybersecurity requires full-time efforts, you can take several steps to better protect your data. Here are a few tips:

Take disaster recovery and backups seriously. Many startups ignore backups and a disaster recovery plan, but these two strategies can greatly reduce the chance that a threat will destroy your business. Create frequent backups and store them in a safe location, with one location being off-site. Separate cloud backups are good for disaster recovery because they are inaccessible to ransomware and malware.

Review compliance standards specific to your industry. Compliance regulations require businesses to have access controls and use specific cybersecurity infrastructure (e.g., firewalls and antivirus). Bringing your environment to compliance standards will help your business avoid hefty fines for violations, and it will give your business a foundation for a good cybersecurity posture.

Consider email security and content filters. Effective email security software will use artificial intelligence to identify malicious messages and block them from being delivered to user inboxes. Web content filters block users from accessing malicious websites that contain malware or phishing content.

Enable monitoring across all network resources. Advanced monitoring and event aggregating tools can be expensive, but most network resources (including cloud infrastructure) have logging capabilities. Monitoring applications will send notifications to administrators after detecting suspicious activity. After a cyber-incident, investigators use event logs to identify vulnerabilities, how a threat was able to compromise the network, and determine if the threat still exists.

Train employees to recognize phishing and other threats. Good cybersecurity requires everyone on board, but most people are unaware of the many ways attackers use phishing and social engineering. Everyone within the organization should have the training, at least annually, as well as routine phishing exercises.

Leverage the cloud when possible. The cloud offers much more cybersecurity infrastructure than what's affordable in-house. Everything from access controls, backups, servers, user management, firewalls, and logging capabilities are available in the cloud, so it makes it easier for small businesses to manage technology especially when administrators are unfamiliar with configuring and managing them.

Install security cameras and alarms if you work from home. It's not uncommon for entrepreneurs to work from home without an office. Any equipment in your home is vulnerable to physical theft, which is just as bad as virtual data theft. Use physical security to protect your computers and devices that contain sensitive data.

Keep all software up to date. Outdated software is a primary vulnerability for many businesses, including small businesses. Developers deploy patches to remediate vulnerabilities in their software, but your business remains vulnerable if you use outdated unpatched software. Keep operating systems and third-party software updated to avoid being a target.

Set up multi-factor authentication (MFA). For employees that fall for phishing and lose their credentials to threats, MFA on all business-critical applications will stop attackers from authenticating into the network. Most email and cloud systems offer MFA capabilities to protect from credential theft.

Encrypt data communications. Any data sent in plaintext can be intercepted and stolen. Any activity on the internet from connecting to the cloud, connecting to a remote machine, to communicating with a website should use encryption. To take it a step further, sensitive data stored on personal devices should be encrypted.

About the Author

As Principal Consultant of Skinner Technology Group, Mike focuses on enabling clients to fully leverage technology investments by providing the insights critical to safeguarding their business, customers' critical data and brand reputation while gaining return on investment from IT. Mike helps clients navigate the challenges of IT operations, cybersecurity, regulatory compliance and business solution implementation.

Mike earned his Bachelor of Accountancy and Master of Accountancy, both with an emphasis in information systems, from the University of Mississippi. He is a Certified Public Accountant in Mississippi and Tennessee and a Certified Information Technology Professional. Mike's lifelong passion for technology has led him to focus his practice on IT and cybersecurity at STG. Mike is a frequent speaker on cybersecurity and IT assurance topics to professional organizations in a wide range of industries. He has a passion for educating users on securing their organizations through sound cyber hygiene practices.

Contact Mike Skinner at:
Website: skinnertechgroup.com

Email: mike@skinnertechgroup.com

Phone: 662.399.2400

LinkedIn: https://www.linkedin.com/in/mtskinnercpa/

Why is Your Small Business a Prime Target for Hackers?

By Patrick Haxton

It seems like every time you turn on the tv, scroll through your social media news feed, or go visit your favorite news website, there is a new story about a company somewhere getting attacked by ransomware or malware or some other form of cyber-attack. They tell you about what happened and what was taken, and sometimes they even tell you how much the company paid in ransom to get back into their systems. So often, business owners read these stories and think to themselves, "I'm glad I am a small company and don't have to worry about getting attacked like these big guys." Then they go about their day, not even considering the thought that they are more at risk than they can ever imagine. Small businesses are at a huge risk.

Let's take a quick journey together. Imagine going into the office Monday morning after a 4-day weekend. You set your things down on your desk and turn on your computer. While it starts to boot up, you walk into the break room and start making a pot of coffee. Other employees start filtering in. Some head to their office to get their day started. A couple come into the break-room at the smell of coffee, and you start chatting about the weekend and ask about how their kids' football game went. Someone pops their head in and says they are having problems accessing files on the server. You tell them you'll take a look at it in a couple of minutes and continue making your coffee. Someone else says they have a funny message on their screen and wants to know who played a prank on them. You think nothing of it and head back to your office to look into the server issue. You log in to your computer, open up your shared drive, and notice all of the file names have been changed and encrypted. You try to open one and it opens a window letting you know that your data has been locked and that if you want it back, you need to follow the payment instructions to release your data. You close it out and open another one. Same thing. As you are doing this, you notice the files on your desktop start to change and suddenly, they are encrypted as well. You hear your other colleagues yelling down the hall that they can't open anything either. Then it begins to sink in. You were hacked.

This was a call that I got on a Monday morning after Thanksgiving. The company wasn't a client. They had googled "cybersecurity" in our town and had come across our website. When she told me what had happened, I gave her a few immediate things she needed to do to make sure nothing spread to other computers, or worse, devices outside their network. I jumped in my truck and headed over to her office. By the time I got there, she had sent 2 of her employees home because there was nothing for them to do. She and her other 2 employees were sitting in silence with stunned looks on their faces. After I introduced myself, the questions from the owner started flowing. Where is my data, and when will I get my data back? How did this happen? Then she asked THE question. Why did they target me? I am just a small 'nobody' company. That is the question that we are going to dive into in this chapter.

If I had a dollar for every time a business owner told me, "I am just a small business. Hackers don't care about me." I could retire to a nice beach somewhere. I always chuckle a little when I hear the question and the person who asked it looks at me with a puzzled look on their face. "Do you want the short version or the long version of why they care about you?" The short answer is that your business is an easy target. In this chapter, we will discuss the long answer and dive into why your small business is a target.

The first reason is that most business owners don't think it will happen to them, so they don't think to take any necessary precautions. You don't know what you don't know. Small companies usually cannot afford to have an internal tech team or IT team. It usually falls on employees or the owner to set up the computers, make decisions about software and apps that are used, and the type of infrastructure installed. Sure, you have some owners who will take the time and learn about technology and learn a little about IT, but most business owners are focused on running their businesses. They don't have time to research all of that, and frankly, they don't want to. If they wanted to learn about those things, they would have opened up a technology company. Oftentimes, the cost is also a factor. So the business owner might look for deals on hardware or maybe purchase subpar hardware because it saves them a little money. With the way cyber-attacks are increasing, things are changing daily. Business owners have to be more educated than ever on the new threat landscape. This doesn't mean they need to go out and take courses on cybersecurity or learn how to do IT. But they do need to be aware that there is a risk, the risk is real, and that risk can be very costly. Making the wrong decision can take a recoverable situation and turn it into a disaster.

One thing we also see when we are performing a Cybersecurity Risk Assessment for prospective clients is just an overall lack of security in the business. This partially ties back to the previous point. Smaller companies cannot afford to have IT or cybersecurity technicians on staff. It is easy to put an ROI on a salesperson or a marketing person or even an employee who is directly performing work for their clients. Sales and billable hours are easy to track. It can be much harder to put an ROI on an IT technician in your company. That role does not directly make the company any money.

Medium to large enterprise businesses usually have larger budgets and can afford to hire an IT technician or put together a team. They can also afford better hardware and better tools, which leads to a better overall security posture. So how does this make a small business more of a target? Hackers know that small businesses don't have the security that the big guys do, making small businesses an easier target. Systems are easier to access. There are more back doors to enter.

There are fewer hurdles to jump through to get into your data. A hacker wants to get into as many systems as quickly as possible, so they make as much money as possible. Does it make sense to target a large company where they might spend hours banging their head on the wall to get in or does it make more sense to target a bunch of little companies that are easy to get in?

If a hacker can compromise enough little companies, in the time it would take to compromise a large company, they still make the same amount of money, and sometimes even more. How many times have you heard someone say, "Work smart, not hard?" Hackers are starting to work smart. I think at this point, everyone has either gotten or knows someone who has gotten the email from the "prince who has died and decided to leave you all of his money." How many times did we laugh and say, "yeah ok...not today Mr. Hacker." Well, you don't see too many of those emails anymore. Why? Because they got smart and have changed their tactics.

Another area we often see small businesses struggle with is online security. When we talk about online security, we are referring to what users are doing online, what they have access to, etc. How many times have you been with a friend who works for a large corporation, and they say something like, "I can't access that website on my company computer," or "they have us locked down and I can't watch that video online." Bigger corporations understand the dangers and they limit what their employees have access to on the internet. As much as people might not like it, corporations aren't limiting what their employees can do online just to be mean or make it more difficult for their people to do their job. Have you ever seen a side view picture of an iceberg? You see this massive iceberg jutting out of the water next to an image or depiction of a ship for size reference. Then you see below the water, that the iceberg is 10 to 20 times bigger. But you can't see that from the surface. If you didn't know anything about icebergs, you wouldn't even know how large it was underwater.

That is how the internet is. The websites you go to, the videos you watch, the endless scrolling on different pages, that is the internet we know. That is the iceberg above the water. So, what is below the waterline in that dark water that we can't see? That is the dark web, the "bad websites," the places where hackers and criminals hang out. It is so much larger than what one would think it is. When a small business doesn't have any restrictions on where their employees go on the internet, it can be really easy to accidentally dip below the water surface. Maybe you are reading a news story and a weird picture catches your eye or you are scrolling social media and see a funny story that you want to read. Next thing you know, you are 4 or 5 websites in from where you started, and you have no idea what bad things could be lurking on those pages. You could have malware or a virus that has downloaded in the background and suddenly your machine is infected. This is why businesses limit where their employees can go on the internet. It is all about online security. We had a client last year who called me and wanted me to talk to one of their employees who was giving them issues about not being able to go where they wanted on the internet. The employee was showing dissent and was on the verge of being let go. They wanted me to try and explain to the employee in a last-ditch effort. I sat down with the employee and let her go on for 10-15 minutes about how she is trustworthy, knows what she is doing, would never click on anything bad, etc. I just sat there and let her go.

Finally, when she was done, she got quiet and looked at me. I asked her if she has any kids. "You know I have two (I've known her awhile and knew her kids were both under the age of 5)." I said, "Are they good kids? Do you trust them?" She said, "Mostly, yes. Occasionally we will have an issue. I can leave them in a room by themselves and not worry about them doing something they aren't supposed to do." I then asked her if she had any baby gates up in her house. She said, "Of course, I do." I asked her why. She responded with, "Just because they know they aren't supposed to go somewhere, doesn't mean they always listen. The baby gate makes sure they don't go there anyway." I just looked at her. You could see the lightbulb go off and she said, "Ahh, I get it now." She got up, went back to her desk, and never complained again.

Earlier in the chapter, we posed the biggest question that I get asked. The second biggest question I get asked is, "What is the biggest risk to my business?" The answer to that is your employees. Now before you start firing everyone, keep reading. It isn't their fault. Why are employees the biggest risk? Because everyone is human, and you don't know what you don't know. Your employee wasn't born knowing how to do their job. You had to train them and teach them. They probably even do continuous education, so they are always learning new things and new ways to accomplish their job and help your company grow. In some fields, this is even mandatory to maintain certifications. So why would we expect that they know how to prevent cyber-attack attempts?

I mentioned earlier that the cybersecurity landscape is changing daily. That means employees need to be educated on the risks that are out there to your business. They need to understand that there are bad people out there that want nothing more than to steal your data and watch your company burn. And even once they do understand those risks, what do you do about it? That is where security awareness training comes in. Security awareness training is something we do ongoing with our cyber clients. We do this in the form of videos, webinars, in-person training, quizzes, evaluations, and phishing campaigns.

These are all things that you, as a business owner, can do to educate your employees. You can have your employees watch short little videos once a week that teach them about ways that hackers try to get in and how to recognize it. You could have someone come in and do a "lunch and learn" with your employees. We have found those work really well. People love to congregate when there is food, especially when it is free.

Phishing campaigns are also a great way to test your employees. If they click all the way through, it will go to a dummy website that lets them know if that had been a malicious email, they would have been compromised. It is also tracked so we can generate a report on who opened the email, who clicked the link, who entered credentials (the credentials are not captured), and how long did they stay on that fake compromised page.

The employee evaluation part of our Cybersecurity Risk Assessment is a huge part. Not only are we doing phishing campaigns, but we interview key employees. We are going to ask questions specific to their role. For the accounting managers, we will ask questions about how they invoice, how they pay invoices, and how money flows in and out of the company. For the C Suite individuals, we want to ask them what role technology plays in the company, what type of security is implemented, do they think your company is at risk for a cyber-attack. We even interview a few people that go all the way down to entry-level.

Oftentimes, management doesn't sit down and talk with them about these things. We ask them questions like what applications do you use, are you allowed to work from home, how do you connect, have there been any security issues while you have been here, and how concerned are you that your company could be hit with a cyber-attack. This question is the big one. So many times, business owners are truly blown away by these answers as they never thought their employees would understand the risk or that their employees care about that risk and the business. These are all questions you can be asking your employees. As a business owner, you need to know who is most at risk of inadvertently furthering an attack, so you can prioritize their training. It isn't their fault that they don't know these things. But once they realize that they don't know, it's up to them to learn how to help make it harder for hackers to gain access to your systems.

The next reason why your business is a prime target is because of your data. When I say your data, you might ask "what does that even mean?" Your data is your information. It is your files. It is everything pertinent to your company. Most small businesses fill a niche role for their clients. Maybe you are a doctor's office. Maybe you are an engineering firm. Maybe you are a small man-ufacturer. No matter what your company does, you are going to have some sort of proprietary information that is relevant to your company and your clients. How does this make you a prime target?

Well, if the nature of your business requires you to have PII (personal identifiable information) for your clients, then that information is valuable because it can be sold to identity thieves and scammers. Maybe your com-pany developed a new product that solves a problem for your client. What would that be worth to your competition? As a medical office, you deal with HIPAA records. What happens if those get out? In most states, there are mandatory reporting requirements if you are breached, and X number of records are compromised.

Not only will they require you to do digital forensics, but often require you to pay for credit monitoring for your clients who were affected. They will even fine you. Some of these fines are daily fines that continually compound until you correct the issues or complete every one of the steps that they require. Also, these fines are not cheap.

Depending upon the type of records that were compromised, some of these fines reach thousands of dollars a day. How many business owners have that kind of capital lying around to pay out? Not only are you looking at fines, fees, and monitoring subscriptions, but because your systems are down, you are not getting any work done. Your expenses have skyrocketed while your revenue is decreasing due to being unable to service clients. What about reputation? Breaches are all published data that is available to the public. When something like this happens, would your clients continue to use your company, or would they look somewhere else for the services you provide?

Another area that businesses don't think about is their accounts, namely their bank accounts. Most banks have commercial accounts that are geared towards small businesses. They have low to no fees on the accounts to help save the business owners money. These are great options for businesses to use, however, they usually don't have the same type of security requirements as the larger corporate checking accounts. So why does this make a difference? In short, they are easy to compromise. Large corporate accounts require check numbers with the amount to be entered into their system for them to be verified and paid. The bank might require a special code to be entered before outside transfers are completed. These restrictions aren't always in place on small business accounts. Remember earlier in the chapter when I talked about hackers getting smart? They are starting to bypass the whole process of locking down your system, demanding a ransom, and hoping you pay it. They are starting to directly target your bank accounts. Why lock your system and hope you pay a ransom when they can gain access to your bank account and take your money directly?

When I talk to small business owners about this, I most often hear, "Well I know my banker, and they wouldn't let something like this happen." Well, it is happening. Every day. Hackers are getting smart. They are compromising your email, learning your habits, and copying your signature and writing style. They can pose as you, start up a conversation with your banker, and the next thing you know, your money is disappearing. If the email looks and sounds exactly like you, would the banker have a second thought about this? Or maybe your company handles a lot of wire transactions. How easy would it be for a hacker to start slipping in fake invoices that your team is used to approving and paying? From the bank's perspective, you are just paying bills like normal. The easiest way, though, is if they just get the login credentials to your bank account. At that point, they have full access and can do anything they want.

Last year, I was helping out a colleague of another small IT firm who had a client that had a breach that resulted in money being wired out of their bank account. Through investigating, we were able to find out that the hackers started by getting into the accounts payable's email address. They waited for that person to go on vacation then emailed the bank as that person and requested the bank add a new admin to the bank account and get online banking credentials set up. The bank emailed back the paperwork. The hackers intercepted the email, printed the documents, forged the signatures (which were almost identical), and emailed them back. The bank went through their process, verifying the person (the hackers used a real name with a real social security number of someone who worked for that company), and emailed the online banking registration details to the "new employee."

The hackers were in their email as well, waiting for those instructions. They took the instructions, set up their own online banking account, and their own security verification text codes, and within minutes, stole over $300,000 out of their primary checking account. Almost instantly, the backend systems of the bank started flagging the checking account and calling the client directly to ask them if all of these were legitimate transactions. At that point, it was too late though. The damage had been done. All of those funds had been wired to different offshore accounts, and that money was never seen again. I'll say it again, hackers are getting smart. They don't have to lock down your systems and demand a ransom to get paid. Think about what is in your business checking accounts right now. What would happen if half of it disappeared? Could your business recover from that? I know what you are thinking. "That is what insurance is for. I have a cyber insurance policy, so I am safe." The truth is you probably aren't. This business I just told you about had a cyber insurance policy.

Do you know how much of that $300,000 they got back? Nothing. It wasn't because coverage had lapsed, or they didn't pay their bill. It was because their claim was denied due to "gross negligence." The insurance company required that MFA (multi-factor authentication) be used on all email accounts. This means every time you sign into your email, your phone gets a code or a notification that for you to approve the login. By the company not having MFA enabled, this was an immediate denial of their claim. When my colleague asked the client why they weren't using MFA on their email accounts, they responded, "It is such a hassle having to put in a code every day when I need to sign into my email." Having MFA would have gone a long way in stopping that hacker from gaining access to their email account and gaining access to their bank accounts.

There are so many more reasons why your small business is a target for hackers. These are some of the big ones. All hope is not lost though! There are things you can do. Hackers are getting smarter, but they still tend to be lazy. If you make it hard for them to get in, they tend to give up and move on to the next company. Remember the company I told you about in the beginning? After they spent a couple of days trying to recover, they decided to pay the ransom (against my recommendation).

The hackers sent them the encryption keys, unlocked their data, and they got back to work. They thought they had dodged a bullet and the nightmare was over. They started the process of interviewing a couple of different cyber companies to start getting their systems up to best practices. Four days later, the same group breached them again, locked their systems, and demanded even more money than the first time. This time, the company didn't pay and decided to try and recover on its own. They lost about half of their client projects, which meant losing the contracts with their clients. They let most of their employees go.

Finally, after about 3 months, they ended up closing the business because they couldn't recover. That was six people who lost their job. Six families were affected. And one small business that had to close its doors. This is just one story, but this happens every day. Business owners don't understand the risk and it is costing them everything. We tell our clients that we are not here to PREVENT you from getting hacked. If a hacker truly wants in, they are going to get in. If this wasn't the case, we would never have large corporations, government entities, etc. getting successfully breached. We won't prevent our clients from getting hacked. Our job is to detect it as it is happening (or as quickly as possible), get them out of the system, and then recover if any damage has been done.

It all isn't bad news, though, because there is light at the end of the tunnel! There are things you can do in your company. Make sure you get a disaster recovery plan in place. Work with your current IT/Cybersecurity consultant (or find one if you don't have one) to build out a plan. Make sure you are using best practices for the software and tools you use. Every one of your software vendors will have security best practices. Make sure you have a solid, stand-alone Cyber Insurance Policy.

When you follow the requirements, they do work, and they are helpful. They will give you a list of things you can be doing as well. Their requirements checklist on the application can be used as a guide. Put training in place for your employees and yourself. Just because you are the business owner, doesn't mean these rules and processes don't apply to you as well. Your employees are watching you. Set the tone. Make this a priority in your company and the culture will flow down from the top. When the employees see how important this is to you, they will take note. You aren't going to change your security posture overnight. It is going to be a process.

But there are little things you can start doing that will make a huge difference. Start with the little, easy things and then move up to the bigger, more difficult things. When I am talking with prospects about this and we get towards the end of the conversation, they all say, "Boy, this sounds expensive. I don't know if I can afford it."

They're right, it can be expensive, but can they afford not to? Can your business afford not to? The hacker targets you because your business and business data do have value, no matter how large or small your company is. It is valuable to YOU. They know this. Their job is to exploit this. By having policies, procedures, training, and tools in place, your company can weather the storm and not become a victim like so many other companies.

About the Author

Patrick Haxton is the CEO and Owner of Preferred Computer Services based in Huntsville Alabama. Preferred Computer Services has been in business since 1991 and provides solutions for businesses to improve their cybersecurity posture through consulting and solution integrations. Business owners should focus on growing their business and not have to worry about the technology aspect. That is where PCS comes in.

Things are constantly changing in the world today, especially in the area of Cyber. Cybercrime is way up and continues to go up every day. Everyone thinks today's hacker is someone in a hoodie sitting in a basement. The reality is that in today's world, there are companies dedicated to hacking that include sales departments, marketing departments, and even 24/7 tech support. Their goal is to trick you into giving them your personal information or even transferring money to them.

Patrick has over 16 years of experience in the IT industry and focuses on helping businesses and their owners understand that today's risk is real, it is high, but it is also addressable. Businesses are having to close their doors every day due to cybercrime. Don't let your business become a statistic.

Contact Patrick Haxton at:

Website: www.Cyber.Pcs-Hsv.com/intro

Email: phaxton@pcs-hsv.com

Phone: 256-513-8206

LinkedIn: LinkedIn.com/in/pcshuntsville/

Cybersecurity Tips for Businesses with Less Than 10 Employees

By Carl de Prado

I enjoy working with small businesses. Regardless of the type of business you are in, you all have one thing in common with other business owners — cybercriminals want to take your money and that of your clients. I have made it my mission to protect small businesses from cybercrime. Cybercriminals come in all sizes, from one-man operations to nation-states. No matter their size and location, they share one goal...harming your business. Small businesses need help as they are one of the biggest targets when it comes to cyber threats. But with the proper steps, small business owners can reduce their risks and not become a statistic.

When it comes to cybercrime,
master Yoda said it best, "Size matters not."

Most small businesses don't think they're big enough to be a target of a cyber-attack. Yet, here are some important facts and statistics you should know if you are a small business with 10 or fewer employees:[4]

Fact #1 – 54% of small businesses think that they're too small to be targeted by cybercrime, but most of the cybersecurity stats we've highlighted indicate that "too small" isn't a consideration for cybercriminals. Think you are not a target because you are not a big organization?

Fact #2 – 43% of cyber-attacks occur against small firms. A few years ago, it was only 18%. Why? Because large organizations have more resources and are becoming more cyber-savvy, fraudsters are targeting smaller businesses. Because they want a business's money, they attack the finance staff.

Fact #3 – 25% of small businesses didn't understand that cyber-attacks cost money, according to Insurance Bee. A quarter of small firms don't comprehend that cybercrime results in large expenses beyond consumer, employee, and company information concerns. A lack of awareness of cyberattack costs may explain why small business owners don't prioritize cybersecurity.

Fact #4 – 60% of small businesses that experience a cyberattack fail within six months, according to the US National Cyber Security Alliance. If a cybercriminal breaches your small business's data, it may close within six months. Cyber-attacks cost a lot of money to recover from. Most small firms can't afford it.

Fact #5 – 47% of small firms don't know how to prevent cyberattacks. Lack of resources and information can make small enterprises vulnerable to cyber-attacks.

Fact #6 – Cyberattacks against small businesses rose 424% last year. This means small business cyber breaches increased more than 5 times last year. Cyber-criminals are swarming small firms. Cybercriminals may target larger organizations since they have more customer data and revenue, right? Not so, it seems.

Fact #7 – Cybercrime costs SMBs more than $2.2 million a year. These expenses can result from cyber-attacks or vulnerabilities, including downtime.

Fact #8 – Ninja RMM says that 3 out of 4 small enterprises lack IT security personnel. This is the biggest difficulty for firms implementing cybersecurity. Even though small businesses said they prioritized cybersecurity and had the budget, they couldn't get the right person.

Fact #9 – 52% of data breaches are caused by human mistakes and technology failure.

Over half of all cybersecurity breaches are caused by human error or system failure, despite popular belief. 48% of data breaches are malicious. While you shouldn't disregard a malicious data leak, you should double down on cyber protection for your own systems and personnel.

Fact #10 – Cybersecurity isn't prioritized in many ways. 83% of small enterprises don't have cyber-attack funds. Savings for a post-cyber-attack response may not count as cybersecurity. Having the cash to manage a data breach will help your firm react swiftly and efficiently.

Fact #11 – Over half of small businesses don't have a cyber-attack plan. 54% of small firms haven't planned for a cyber-attack, per Insurance Bee.

Fact #12 – Small and mid-sized firms averaged $955,429 to return to normal following a cyber assault. The average firm polled had $879,582 stolen. The expense of returning back to normal far exceeds the money stolen in a cyber-attack.

Fact #13 – Understanding how a cyber-attack happened is key to responding effectively. This might cost over $25,000, regrettably. Finding and fixing a cyber breach's vulnerability is crucial for moving forward and protecting your firm from future assaults, but it will cost you.

Fact #14 – Black Stratus and other experts advise organizations to invest at least 3% of their budget in cybersecurity. If you're not investing this much in cybersecurity, you're missing a critical safeguard.

Although the above stats aren't exactly uplifting, they're just the reality of owning a small business. Here are some steps you can take to ensure that your small business doesn't become just a number in the broader scheme of small business cybercrime.

Steps to Protect Your Business

The first and most important first step is to turn on Multi-Factor Authentication (MFA).

Why is an MFA necessary?

Your organization's security will be bolstered by MFA since users will be required to prove their identity through more than just their username and password.

Brute force assaults may easily crack usernames and passwords, making them valuable targets for hackers. Using an MFA element like a fingerprint or a real hardware key increases your organization's confidence that it will remain safe from cybercriminals.

Exactly how does an MFA work?

MFA is able to function by requiring more information to be verified (factors). One-time passwords are one of the most typical MFA factors that consumers encounter (OTP). One-time passwords (OTPs) are codes that are sent to your mobile device via email, SMS, or a mobile app. OTPs generate a new code every time an authentication request is made, or every time a new code is generated. Some other aspect, such as an incremented counter, or a time value, is used to generate the code. This is done when the user initially registers.

The bad guys can't do anything if you have MFA on, even if they acquire your password.

Passwords

You don't want to use the same password for more than one site. If the website is breached, all of the usernames and passwords are released to the public. There have been many, many, attacks and breaches that makeup millions and millions of records. The bad guys take these and sell them on the dark web for fun and profit.

The bad guys can also do credential stuffing, where one account's data is obtained by the cybercriminals, and they attempt to use the same credentials on other websites that have potential value such as banks.

The best solution for this is a password manager. There are many on the market such as LastPass, Keeper, Passportal, and several others. They all work under the same premise. You learn one password to the password vault, which is a cloud-based service. A good password manager such as LastPass, will not even save that password so that if breached, the bad guys couldn't get into the vault.

Tip: Don't put passwords on stickies or underneath the keyboard. I would put it inside of a book that you read or behind a picture on the wall. That way, if your office is breached, the bad guys would not likely be looking in a book for a password.

Dark Web Monitoring

Dark web monitoring is looking for and keeping track of personal information on a part of the internet that most people can't get to.

The dark web is a secret network of websites that can only be accessed by using a special web browser. It can't be found by search engines, and users can hide their IP addresses by using it. Because of its privacy and anonymity, the dark web is a place for people who want to stay hidden, whether it's for a good reason or because they're committing a crime, such as identity theft.

If someone gets your Social Security number or other identifying information, they might try to sell it on the dark web to someone who wants to use it to commit fraud. Monitoring the dark web can help you protect your identity and, by extension, your finances.[5]

Back-Up and Test Your Data

If you are the victim of ransomware, a good reliable backup can save the day. Whatever data your business needs to run needs to be backed up regularly and tested. How many places do you need to keep your data? Typically, three places — the original, a local copy, and an off-site location — just depending upon the data.[6]

The "rule of three" for backing up business data is a useful idea. It became well-known because photo-grapher Peter Krogh used it to keep his pictures safe. Even though it comes from photography, the "backup rule of three" is often seen as good advice. The idea reminds businesses how many backup files to keep and where to keep them.

The "three-backup rule" says that you should:

1. Make at least three copies of your data.

2. Keep the copies on at least two types of media.

3. Keep at least **one of those copies offsite**.

Three copies - you should have at least three copies of your data, including the one in your live environment. This means that if something goes wrong, you will always have backups. We would suggest making copies at least once a day. But it's better if you can make as many copies as you can.

Two types of media - use at least two different kinds of media to protect against hardware failure. Tape drives, hard drives, and the cloud are all ways to do this. It is best to make sure you use both internal storage and a removable (or offsite) alternative. There shouldn't be any connection between the two. So, if one fails, the other will still work.

One copy offsite - keep a copy of your data somewhere else. Don't put that copy with the rest of your data. This is to keep you safe from the worst disasters. For example, flooding could damage your whole business, making your on-site data storage inaccessible and impossible to fix.

The Three-Backup Rule and the Cloud

The rule of three backups can be hard to follow, but it is a best practice. For instance, removable hard drives are an alternative type of media that you can take offsite. But removable hard drives are easy to damage or lose, so cloud-based backup solutions can help. These services offer a safe alternative to local storage media. The cloud uses data centers that are not at your business, so they won't fail if something goes wrong at your business. Because of this, data centers are a more reliable way to keep data safe than other methods.

If you want to follow the rule of three backups, the cloud is a good way to do it.

Anti-Virus

Your anti-virus isn't cutting it anymore. Years ago, the only thing most small businesses needed to do to be safe online was to install antivirus and call it a day. Those days are gone, and just like a whip and buggy, they are never coming back. Antivirus software is a type of program designed and developed to protect computers from malware like viruses, computer worms, spyware, botnets, rootkits, keyloggers, and such. Antivirus programs function to scan, detect and remove viruses from your computer. The problem with antivirus software is that it needs to be updated regularly for new virus threats. The updates contain files on the latest known viruses. The problem arises if the virus software is not known.

Hackers have known about and found many ways to circumvent common antiviruses.[7]

Compromised Devices

With the rise of smartphones, tablets, and laptops, network security is less regulated by antivirus software. BYOD programs let workers bring their own gadgets to work.

Businesses may protect against BYOD vulnerabilities by tightening network security, upgrading to a dedicated firewall service, and correcting security gaps. Use a company-approved app to scan new and old devices for malware and viruses.

Home users can't prohibit hacked devices from entering their network as easily. We can't tell visitors how essential network and system security is, so we can only hope they're savvy and aware of hazards. But this is not always the case.

Insider Threats

Along with BYOD, an insider threat could harm your network by accessing it. Someone inside your company may be able to surprise you and your coworkers. Insider dangers include:

- Malicious insiders are rare but have the most damage-causing power especially if they are administrators.

- Insiders are often deceived or compelled to give out information or credentials.

- Insiders are often careless and click without thinking, opening phishing emails that appear as if they originated from their firm.

- Insider threats are challenging to protect against because there's no consistent behavior pattern that indicates an attack. An attacker's motivations vary.

- IP theft is taking intellectual property without authorization.

- Espionage is gathering secret or sensitive information about an organization to gain an advantage or coerce someone.

- Fraud involves stealing, altering, or disseminating personal or business information.

- Sabotage is damaging a system from within.

People in and out of the office have easier access to crucial information and systems, as well as many opportunities to leak information. Therefore, trust becomes the most critical aspect of security, and antivirus software becomes endpoint backup. "The U.S. economy has altered in 20 years. Intellectual capital, not physical assets, drives most of a U.S. company's worth. This makes spying on corporate assets easier."

Understanding the threat landscape is simply one component of addressing insider threats.

Advanced Persistent Threats (APT)

APTs sometimes go undiscovered because they wait to attack. Malware or viruses could be installed weeks or months before activation. They wait for remote control instructions. APTs are usually the work of a team of highly trained, professional hackers who may be backed by a nation-state.

When a bad actor utilizes an APT, they try to steal intellectual property, classified or sensitive information, trade secrets, financial data, or anything else that could injure or blackmail the target(s).

APTs include Remote Access Trojans (RAT). When activated, the malware package allows a remote controller to acquire as much data as possible before being identified. Finding them is difficult. RATs usually have complex network protocols to communicate with remote controllers. Once a communication channel is established, no malware or malicious code is communicated. This implies antivirus and firewall software are clueless.

Finding APTs can be difficult. You might notice late-night logins rise, or a sudden surge in administrator access late at night. These could be a symptom of an ongoing operation if your personnel is occupied during the day.

APT hackers may have planted Trojans throughout the local network, enabling them access to your machine if their main point of attack is detected. You clean one system, but they have access to the next.

Signs of APT's include:

- Unknown sources send large or unexpected data transfers to an unknown or unfindable address.

- Unexpected data collections or data clusters. It may have been saved in an unpopular archive format.

- Spear-phishing efforts increased. Check the other signals if someone unintentionally clicked.

You need to know how your data flows to recognize an attempted or ongoing ATP attack, thus it's worth your effort to learn about your network.

Viruses & Malware

Attackers are now very savvy. An attacker will test a new malware against both simple and advanced antivirus software before releasing it. Why make malware, secure their identities, and provide a variety of attack channels if they'll be shot down immediately?

After three-quarters of decline, Q4 saw 42M new malware samples. Despite fluctuating numbers, growth and relevance are real. Malware developers constantly release new code. They modify their programs to exploit new security weaknesses before they're corrected.

So, what do you do to protect your computers?

Using an MDR Service

Managed detection and response (MDR) is an out-sourced service that helps companies find threats and deal with them when they are found. This is the best course of action.[8]

Security providers give their MDR customers access to their team of security researchers and engineers. These people are in charge of keeping an eye on networks, figuring out what happened, and fixing security cases. MDR tries to solve some of the most important problems that modern businesses face. The most obvious problem is that most organizations don't have enough people with security skills. Larger companies that can afford it may be able to train and set up dedicated security teams that can hunt for threats full-time. However, most companies won't be able to do this because they don't have enough resources. This is especially true for medium-sized and large organizations, which are often the targets of cyber-attacks but don't have the money or people to put together teams to stop them.

Use the Spam Email/Web Gateway Security Service[9]

How do Secure Email Gateways Function and How Can They Help Your Organization?

Businesses benefit from secure email gateways. They protect employees from spam, malware, and phishing, protecting organizations. Email is one of the best ways for hackers to access employees and attack business networks through employees. Secure email gateways protect employees against fraudulent emails and phishing assaults.

Secure email gateways also help businesses meet compliance standards. Many secure email gateways offer email archiving and encryption to secure sensitive data and meet compliance requirements by retaining correspondence for legal reasons. Businesses can be both secure and legal.

Cybersecurity Awareness Training and Phishing Tests[10]

Why should employees receive security training?

Human mistakes cause 90% of security breaches, according to research. Training reduces risk, reducing loss of PII, IP, money, or brand reputation. Effective cybersecurity awareness training addresses mistakes employees may make with email, online, and in the physical world, such as tailgating or incorrect document disposal.

Increase security using phishing testing

Mimecast Awareness Training makes it easy to test phishing emails. You can deploy a phishing template to users in about 10 minutes.

How should awareness training be conducted?

Engaging today's employees in security awareness training reduces user risk. Many security awareness programs neglect education best practices, delivering one-off sessions that overload consumers or are forgettable. Training must be offered consistently in tiny doses to fit employees' hectic schedules. Positive reinforcement and humor boost security subject retention more than fear-based or dull messaging.

Cybersecurity Risk Assessment

Before a company can improve its cybersecurity, it needs to know what its processes, procedures, or implementations are vulnerable to and what threats they face. These threats could be common ways that hackers attack, operational risks, or risks that are specific to a certain industry.[11]

To better understand how important risk assessment is in business, you need to be familiar with what are risk assessments for, and what should be in a risk assessment?

By doing a risk assessment, weaknesses can be found and put into groups. Some organizations, like those that have to follow HIPAA, may have to do periodic risk assessments in order to stay in compliance.

Does it look like a lot of things need to be done to protect your business? In a word, yes. When you start down the road of protecting your company it can seem like inhaling water from a high-pressure hose. Don't despair, many business owners are putting these practices into place and reaping the rewards of being able to sleep at night knowing their company data is safe, their company's image is impeccable, and their team is effective and stays loyal. You can too by implementing what we just covered.

About the Author

Carl de Prado has over 30 years of experience in the Cybersecurity and Information Technology industries. In 2006 Carl started A2Z Business IT, a cybersecurity firm located 25 miles north of Manhattan serving the Metro New York Area.

Carl specializes in helping clients keep their data secure in the financial sector with a focus on M&A, Private Banking, and Insurance.

One of the most exciting case studies was helping a client stop an internal embezzlement scheme that prevented over half a million dollars of loss.

Carl always looks to help the Cybersecurity Community; one of the ways is as a mentor to other IT companies thru the ASCII Spark Program and as an active member of InfraGard. InfraGard is a unique partnership between the Federal Bureau of Investigation (FBI) and individuals in the private sector for the protection of U.S. critical infrastructure and the American people.

Besides being a husband to Sophia (wife) and a father to Mackenzie (daughter) and Benjamin (son) Carl enjoys hiking and nature photography, crafts, and graphic novels based on art from 1950 to the 1970s.

The key to Carl's success is he has dedicated his life to making sure his client's environments are protected and functioning properly. Carl takes pride in the care that is unparalleled in the industry. Carl makes it easier for his clients to sleep at night knowing that their data is secure, their company's image is impeccable, and their team is effective and stays loyal.

If you would like to learn more about how Carl can help your company, feel free to book a call for a free cyber review at:

booking.a2zbusinessit.com.

If you have a cybersecurity Issue, feel free to reach out to Carl's team 914-350-3744, or scan the QR code.

Eight Essential Strategies That You Need to Implement

By Dean Elliott

What is a Cyber-Attack?

A Cyber-Attack is any attempt to steal, expose, change, restrict access to or destroy information through unauthorised access to a computer system.

Cyber-attacks can happen in many different ways and by now you will have likely heard of the most common. These days terms like Trojan, Phishing, Malware, and Ransomware are in everyone's vocabulary, but do you know what can happen because of these breaches?

Consider this one example: Jane is the receptionist at your busy real estate company, spending all day emailing and taking phone calls. One day Jane receives a notice that she needs to log in to her email again, so she clicks the link and is presented with the email provider's login page, where she enters her password and carries on working. She is very busy, and everything keeps working, so this event is immediately forgotten. She wouldn't even think it worthwhile to mention it to you.

Jane has just fallen victim to a phishing attack. In fact, it was not the email provider's login page; it was an exceptionally good copy made by an attacker and now the attacker has access to her email. She often receives applications for rental properties and has follow-up emails with your customers about potential sales or even supplier invoices via email. All these emails contain a lot of confidential information — a goldmine for the attacker who can sell this information on the dark web!

The attacker may also leverage this to gain further access throughout your business, possibly into your company data or your email. The power they would have while being able to send email as the "big boss" is staggering.

On average it would take 287 days to contain this breach.[12] Imagine the amount of information the attacker could gather or the destruction that could be caused in that time!

Why implement E8?

The immediate damage could be theft of money directly from your accounts or all of the data you need to operate being locked so you can't access it. Additionally, the impact of an attack may not be immediately obvious and may have longer-lasting negative effects on your business. For example, your clients may lose confidence in your ability to keep their information safe and choose to use another provider.

Once a breach is detected, you may be required by law to report it to your regulatory body. In Australia, this is known as the Notifiable Data Breach Scheme (NDB) and requires that breaches be reported to the Office of the Australia Information Commissioner (OAIC).

People often ask me, and all too often, after an attack occurs, "Can't I do something to prevent this from happening?" And the answer is "YES! Of course!"

The Australia Cyber Security Centre (ACSC) has released the Essential Eight[13] which is a framework for protecting businesses from Cyber-Attacks. These eight strategies are split across three primary objectives – Prevent Attacks, Limit Attack Impact, and Data Recoverability.

You might be saying to yourself, "But I'm not in Australia." That doesn't matter. Although the Essential Eight is unique to Australia, the framework is a useful baseline that all businesses should implement to pro-tect themselves from Cyber-Attacks.

What are the Eight Essential Strategies?

1. Application Control

The purpose of an Application Control strategy is to limit the applications that are allowed to run in your business. Think about all the programs you need to use in your day-to-day business and add them all to a list. Think Word, Excel, Chrome, Outlook, MYOB, Quick-Books, and even things like the Calculator app or your calendar. Now, once you have this list, let's tell the com-puter that these applications are okay to run, and every-thing else is blocked. That's Application Whitelisting.

Application Whitelisting is a robust strategy for protecting computers against malicious applications. If a dodgy program is blocked by default, then it can't do any damage. There is an added bonus here that staff can't install games or their own time-wasting programs to your computers either. So, no lost time cleaning up slow computers with all the extra junk they put on there and it also cuts off one avenue in which staff can be unproductive.

This is likely to be the most difficult of all the strategies to implement but certainly one that is well worthwhile implementing properly. A properly configured whitelist will prevent a significant amount of basic and sophisticated attacks on your business.

2. Patch Applications

There is a constant battle between the good guys and the bad guys. The bad guys are continually trying to find new ways to sneak into systems to perform their nefarious activities while the good guys are battling to stop them.

Vulnerabilities in applications are one way that the bad guys can gain access to a system, which is why it is important to keep everything up to date. Once a vulnerability is discovered, the application vendor usually fixes this as a matter of urgency and will release an update or patch. By ensuring you keep systems and applications up to date, you are ensuring you have the best protection against the most recent holes that attackers have found to exploit.

"But isn't this automatic?" Well, yes, they are meant to be, but quite often the automatic update functions fail without notification. If someone isn't checking whether updates are successful, chances are likely that some computers in your business are not updated. Some of these won't have an automatic update function and some will require you to pay for updates. Not doing these updates can leave you vulnerable.

How about the software that you only use to do that one infrequent task, but you can't update it because you can't justify the cost of the upgrade, but you also can't get rid of it? These situations happen, and if you take the necessary steps to keep that computer safe, then okay. This is best done by unplugging it from the internet. Don't allow unpatched applications or computer access to the internet.

3. Office Macro Settings

Macros are designed to automate routine tasks in Office to help improve the workflow and usability of a document. They are a powerful tool and can be especially useful when put in the right hands. Unfortunately, this also means they are a powerful tool for hackers to use as well. A macro can be used to execute malicious code on your computer simply by opening a seemingly benign document.

A common attack method is to send a doc file to you via email and call it something like "Invoice 2673.pdf.doc" so it looks like a PDF file, but it's not. If you open this file, a macro would run and deploy the malicious code, often ransomware. Most people who use email have seen this at some point and may have been lucky to just delete it. You probably have seen this one yourself. I hope you deleted it and didn't witness the nasty effects it could have on your computer.

As macros are a powerful way to streamline repetitive business tasks, you may need to use them and will not be able to block all of them. For example, you may have a macro that runs in Excel to process your monthly payroll or in a Word document to pre-fill customer details from a list. You will need to identify these macros and whether they are required in your business. If you can migrate the macros functions to another method, do that and block all macros. If it is not possible, at least in the short term to migrate, then restrict access to only essential macros. Also, restrict access to only the computers that need to use macros.

If you don't have a specific business case for using macros, then the settings should be set to block all.

4. Application Hardening[14]

Application hardening is something that we should do when first bringing a new application into the business environment. It needs to be tested so you know that it works and does so securely. We don't want any new application opening a hole in your internal network.

Often the supplier of the software will have a hardening guide for you to follow to best set up your new program.

The default settings are often at the most permissive, so you should really explore all the options to make sure you restrict the program to only what it needs to access, and who needs to access it.

Legacy applications may rely on older software or require the use of an old browser. This is not a good idea as they are not patched, and vulnerabilities are common. It is very easy for a bad actor to obtain an exploit kit to take advantage of your unpatched applications allowing them access to the systems.

Common examples of these are Adobe Flash, Java, Silverlight, Microsoft Office, PDF Viewers, and Internet Explorer. If you don't have any legacy applications in your network that require these programs, great! Let's block them all to stay secure.

You should configure all web browsers to block Flash, Java, Silverlight, and advertisements. These old programs can't do any harm if they are blocked. If you can remove them from your computers as well as block them from being installed, that is best.

Microsoft Office applications and PDF Viewers should be prevented from creating child processes. If you open a Word document, you aren't likely going to want it to spawn a bunch of other variations of itself. These could be mutated and used to run malicious code. It's safer just to block it.

There are lots of things that can be done to harden applications and they will vary from app to app. That's why it's always best to consult the guide from the vendor.

Just consider what the application does, and what data it has access to. Construct your policies around limiting its access to only what it needs but also limiting access to the application or securing the methods that users can access the application.

Application hardening is not a set-and-forget task either, you must revisit these policies and verify that what was once secure is still secure. I suggest a review every 6 -12 months.

5. Restrict Admin Privileges

Admin privileges are the highest, unmitigated access you can get in a system. These can live in three levels, Local (just the computer), Domain (all computers and servers on a network), or Global (all computers and servers as well as cloud apps). The potential that these credentials unlock for a bad actor is what makes them the highest target and why it is never a good idea for any user to have these privileges.

Admin privileges should be reserved for a separate admin user. I know of many bosses who think that they, or even some of their managerial staff, should have admin privileges. They think that they are the boss, and they should not be disallowed anything on their systems. While I agree with that, the owner of the business should have access to anything they want BUT it should not be their main user account. Generally, it isn't something that the business owner needs to know and should be left to IT.

If your user account is the administrative user, then you become a higher risk and a greater target. Admins should be a separate user, and the credentials securely stored, not something that is easily remembered or accidentally entered or captured by bad actors.

Limit privileged access to those who absolutely need it. It may not be a bad actor who steals credentials to do damage to your business-critical systems. If an employee who has privileged access unknowingly changes settings or deletes something, that can be devastating to a business.

Recently, I have seen exactly this happen. A user was having a "clean up" before getting rid of an old computer. This user deleted all the company data from the Shared Drive because it wasn't needed on their computer anymore. They did not realise that the deletion synced across all computers in the business. They weren't trying to do anything harmful, but it still happened. Fortunately, there was a backup, but it still took days to get the business operating again.

6. Patch Operating Systems

For all the same reasons I mentioned for patching applications, the Operating System is possibly even more important. Most people know and do allow Windows or macOS to update automatically, but very few are checking this. So, when the automatic update fails, no one knows and it just doesn't get done, leaving it vulnerable.

Also true for the servers, those operating systems need to be kept up to date but as users rarely interact with the server it goes unnoticed. Unless your IT provider is actively patching and updating your servers, they are likely quite out of date. I often find servers, many years (years!) out of date when conducting an audit for a new client.

Another thing that shocks me still is how many com-puters are still running Windows 7. Being retired way back in 2020, it hasn't had any updates for many years. If you have this in your environment, please do some-thing about it. I saw one 12-year-old computer running Windows 7 just the other day that held all the business data and had no backup. It terrifies me.

7. Multi-Factor Authentication

This one strategy has got to be my favourite or maybe equal favourite to Application Whitelisting. It is such a simple yet super effective way to prevent an attacker from accessing an account. You likely already use this on some of your accounts.

If you don't know, Multi-Factor Authentication (MFA) or Two Factor Authentication (2FA) is another step in the login process that challenges the user to enter a code

(SMS, email, mobile app or phone calls are common) before the login attempt is granted. So even if the bad actor has your password, they can't log in without this extra authentication method.

While having any kind of MFA is preferable to having no MFA on an account, not all MFA controls are created equal. Some are more secure than others. The more secure controls require a separate hardware token, bio-metrics, or a physical One-Time-Pin token.

Already some accounts, like Microsoft 365, allow the login without passwords and it's simpler and more secure than having a password! Just put in the USB token and enter your PIN, and you're logged in rather than entering your email and password with the code SMSed to you. I'm looking forward to seeing many more providers adopting this option in the future.

This is probably a good time to mention Password Managers. Don't use the same password for all your accounts. Even with MFA, this is bad practice. Having random, different passwords for every account you own is what's necessary, but it's impossible to remember all of these. That's where a password manager comes in.

It is a secure way to easily store and recall the password for all your accounts. They have apps that work with your phone or computer so it will automatically enter your password when you log in. Some will even store the MFA code too, making login even simpler. They will even help you generate a new password for a new account you are creating or updating an old password.

8. Regular Backup

The final piece to this puzzle is backup. So, we have stopped programs from running that aren't on our allowed list, macros are disabled, the OS and all the apps are patched, we are using good passwords and MFA, and we have restricted the admin access. Great! But a new Zero-Day exploit is discovered, and it allows the bad actor to bypass one of your security measures and now your data is encrypted! What do we do?

Even though we have all the protections in place to prevent an attack from happening in, it is still possible. So, we need to plan for this, just in case.

Backups should include whole system states, all the business-critical data, and any applications used. Back-ups can take many forms; some people have hard drives or tapes that get changed over every day. These are stored in a vault or taken offsite. Some people prefer to sync all data to a cloud.

It doesn't matter how your backup works as long as there are multiple backup processes and restore pro-cesses. At least one copy of the backup must be stored in a separate geographic location. The backup must happen at least daily. Backups should contain at least 3 months of recovery points, and this should be tested at least every three months.

Although the focus of this is on business, I think it's important to also implement these controls in your personal life as well. Unfortunately, there have been many times when someone was in tears because their phone or computer had died, and it was the only place they had all their baby photos saved. Backup is super important at home too!

Get cracking!

Your business isn't going to protect itself. Just like physical security where you lock the doors and install a burglar alarm — you don't know if anyone is actually going to try to break in. Somebody might be coming to your door each night and trying to pick the lock. You may never know. The same is true for Cyber-Attacks, except it's not just nighttime, it's all the time.

You may like to think it isn't happening to you or your business just because it hasn't yet. But this is a foolish idea and is one that will lead to the lesson being learned the hard way. It's far better to educate yourself and protect your business before someone breaks in.

All of the strategies can be implemented by you, the business owner, and there are tools out there that can help you do so. Although, if you are like most of the business owners I deal with, you have very little time and don't want to do this alone, so you need help. That's totally OK. Look to enlist the help of a Managed Security Service Provider or MSSP and they will be able to make this whole process happen for you.

If your current IT provider isn't pushing for these strategies to be implemented, speak to them about it or speak to another provider who will. After all, it's your business that's on the line so get cracking!

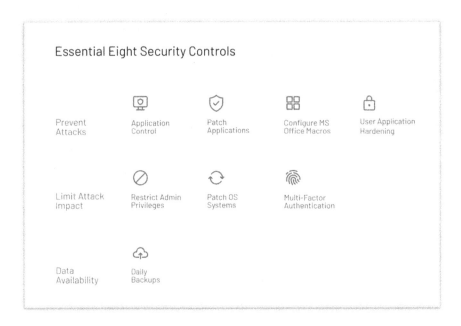

Essential Eight Security Controls

Prevent Attacks	Application Control	Patch Applications	Configure MS Office Macros	User Application Hardening
Limit Attack Impact	Restrict Admin Privileges	Patch OS Systems	Multi-Factor Authentication	
Data Availability	Daily Backups			

About the Author

From an early age, Dean Elliott had always had a keen interest in computers and technology. He could often be found dismantling his parents' old computers to find out how they worked, putting them back together, and getting them to work in all sorts of weird ways. After getting numerous secondary and tertiary qualifications, he got a job with a local IT business in Dunsborough. He then spent the next 10 years increasing his knowledge, honing his skills, and learning new skills in business and IT infrastructure.

In 2016 Dean stepped outside of his comfort zone to start his own company, Elliotts Tech. The primary goal of Dean's new venture was to manage businesses' total IT needs. As cyber threats have been steadily increasing and attacks are becoming significantly more common, and devastating, protecting Elliotts Tech's customers from these threats has become a priority focus for Dean and his team. Now, most days are spent researching risks, cyber protections, and the ever-changing business IT best practices. Dean and his expertly qualified technicians then distill this down into byte-size information that is relevant, pertinent, and can be easily understood by their clients.

As a partner, father, and owner of a growing business, Dean's free time is at a premium. Where possible, he does enjoy spending time participating in charity car rallies, camping, and getting out in the bush with his motorbike or 4x4.

Contact Dean Elliott at:

Website: https://elliotts.tech

Email: Dean@elliotts.tech

Phone: 08 9756 7273

LinkedIn: www.linkedin.com/in/dean-elliotts-tech

Facebook: https://facebook.com/elliottstech

What Your Business Needs to Do to Keep Your Remote Workers Safe from Hackers

By Troy Solis

"Things have changed." This is a term I have heard, and said, a lot lately. In the world of technology, these three words mean so much, and things just keep changing! Cybersecurity attacks are way up, but why? Why do we say the three words? In my opinion, it is because of "Ease" and "Ignorance." I'll explain.

Ease - It's is easy for hackers, of any skill level, to infiltrate many businesses and get them where it hurts... Financially.

Ignorance – Sadly, most small businesses are not aware of the amount of risk their business has! They're confident they are protected. Some feel, "I've got nothing of value on my computers, who cares if I get hacked?" On the other end of the spectrum, you may think, "My IT department has everything taken care of." Both are assumptions. Trust and verify is what my wonderful wife says, time and time again. The same can hold true in the world of cybersecurity.

For many small and medium-sized businesses, their remote workers allow more risks than one might think. In this chapter, we'll discuss how "all businesses" can accomplish implementing a cybersecurity practice that will include remote workers.

Your IT department, an IT service provider, your IT guy, or your brother (who "knows computers") typically focuses on business productivity by keeping technology running, safe from viruses & malware, and able to restore from backup. Those were the days; this is known as "old school" IT management. On the flip side, large corporations have the resources to do much more. Their controls and processes keep the company secure, and always running no matter where their end users may sit, may it be a coffee shop, home office, or a pontoon on a lake. Don't we all deserve to be able to work confidently and securely like a big business? I believe we can. It has been done and my company, like many other technology service providers, is driven to ensure this happens for each of our customers.

My experience is within the medical device manufacturing industry, mostly with startups where small company size is typical. I've built many new networks from the ground up and managed many users and their ability to keep working using technology. Not until the last several years could the small business work remotely in a secure manner. But, are the typical VPNs, proxy servers, anti-virus, and anti-malware software, enough? The problem is that not only do we need to protect the computer systems and the data they contain, but we must also protect the cloud services that our end users have access to. We all have cloud services, whether we know it or not, and we have access to personal and business email accounts, bank accounts, cloud storage, online customer databases. I can keep going, but what are we doing to stay secure?

First, a company must implement a solid set of security policies. A well-defined set of security policies helps get the entire company on the same page and ensures the best available measures are being used appropriately. Some policies must be agreed upon by the end user, specifically, a "bring your own device" (BYOD) policy. Agreement to this policy by the employee allows the company's IT team to set up the appropriate security features on personally-owned devices including computers and mobile phone devices. The alternative to this is the company provides the devices and services to the employee or contractor, so they can be managed and secured by the IT team. This is important. Every device, those that are remote and those in the main office, can be a risk. Not holding the company and its end users accountable for keeping the company's assets secure is a sure path to being hacked.

Your company must review each security policy regularly by your CISO, CIO, or a professional security consultant. This should be done at least annually in order to keep up with the ever-changing world of technology we live in.

When was the last time an assessment has been done on your infrastructure? Since things are always changing, it's important to regularly assess your business systems and end users for security risks at least once every 2 years. This gives you the opportunity to identify security gaps and put together a plan to plug them.

Anti-virus, anti-malware, firewall, computer updates... Wow, things have changed, haven't they? Besides backup and restore capabilities, these tools are enough to protect your business, right? As much as I miss how easy it was to make sure these were in place and maintained, the answer is NO! It is not that easy, hackers don't need to deploy malware, and their motive is not to cause business productivity loss. The overall goal is to steal information and sensitive data to sell on the Dark Web or to gain access to sites that contain financial information. What is sensitive information? Social Security numbers, driver's license numbers, passwords, healthcare information, and email addresses too! This type of information can be found by hackers no matter what device you're using or where you are using them.

This means it is time to expand your security tool stack. What your business includes will end up being expansive, and may include in various ways, the following:

1. Advanced anti-virus/anti-malware protection called Next Gen Anti-Virus.

2. Advanced email protection provides email security that helps prevent phishing attacks, monitoring, and email encryption.

3. Security operations center (SOC).

4. Monitoring and reporting.

5. Password Management, and centralized authentication services.

6. 2-factor and/or multi-factor authentication.

7. DNS filtering, and web content filters.

8. Security information and event management (SIEM) and threat detection.

9. Advance firewall or NextGen firewall.

10. LAN Zero Trust.

11. Backup and recovery

12. Regularly test restore of your backups

13. Vendor management

14. ...and much more

Most importantly, the security stack must be applied to all employees, contractors, and consultants, whether they are remote or working in the office using your systems. Your security policies will help keep things consistent. This all seems very overwhelming. After an assessment, your security team will have a better understanding of the business's security posture and curate a solution that fits your business needs. You may also have compliance requirements. The security tools required to meet your compliance needs will all be revealed during your security assessment.

A good remote working environment will also include quality internet service with quality wireless capabilities. Most large businesses do help to ensure a stable and fast internet service. But they may not ensure their worker can function from any location which is what remote working is all about. Anywhere can include the employee's kitchen table and a patio that is further away from the home office's wireless router. Wireless connectivity can vary from space to space from the wireless router. This is not just the employer's responsibility, it's also the employee and the internet service provider's responsibility, but mostly the employees.

However, the employer's IT department can help. If you're having internet connection issues, communicate with your IT department or IT service provider. Some adjustments can be made by working in tandem with the internet service provider to correct wireless signaling that can improve your wireless connection's consistency. Ideally, work on a cabled ethernet connection when you can, but with remote working now such a common thing, we all expect to be able to work from a wireless connection, so let your IT team help.

A secure wireless connection is a connection that includes a password when first connected to a wireless signal. The wireless device's security protocols will take over from there. When working from a remote location, there are other things to consider regarding connection and security. Wired or wireless connections both have access to the internet and your remote worker may use their computer for personal reasons. A standard business VPN only protects the computer's connection from the public internet while the VPN is on. So, an always-on VPN is required, one that cannot be turned off, or bypassed with a free VPN service. Of course, this is a centrally managed service and should be part of your security stack, always on, and cannot be removed. Many VPNs services of this type will have additional security features. The more the merrier!

Training. No matter where your workers are using the technology provided by your company, the biggest risk to any business is your people! Train, hold them accountable to it, and train again. Each employee should understand your security policies, and how to operate day-to-day with a security-first mindset, and you'll find that training is one of the best things to add to your security stack. It's not only about how to identify a phishing email or websites that are questionable. The employees should keep a clean desk from passwords, and private or secret information, ensure they learn how or when to use secure data storage, learn about data backups, avoid crypto mining, and learn about GDPR regulations such as privacy and security rules and processes. There are many other topics every computer user should understand. Not taking the opportunity to learn as much as we can about cybersecurity only helps the hackers. Learn, learn and learn more. That's how we battle the hackers that have nothing better to do but steal information.

Working remotely, or in the office, access to your IT / Cybersecurity support services should not be hard. If you are afraid to call for support, then why do you hire them? They're there to help, they want to help. They all want to protect the customers from threats and keep each end user working to grow your business. If you're reading this, hopefully, you're not experiencing a dysfunctional relationship with your IT service team. Don't be afraid to change providers. It might hurt at first, but in the long run, when you find that "perfect" team to meet your needs, your company will grow, and hopefully, your IT team will grow with you keeping your business top of mind at all times with a customer-first mindset. Access to a good ticket and training portal will make it easy to not just submit tickets but to monitor them as well as projects. Your support team may even be able to provide "how-to" training materials to help learn how to better use the technology you and your IT team are providing. Any resource that helps your end-users be more secure, and efficiently use technology, will help your business grow and meet your business goals.

All this information can help get your employees on the same page. Although the topic of this chapter is about keeping your remote workers safe from hackers, the security practice applies to the entire business, remote or in the office. The solutions should be a comprehensive and continuous practice. A good security posture with security policies that set the path, security training that increases awareness, a complete security stack, and knowledge of how the security stack helps mitigate business risks, will get you there.

Get started as soon as you can, but be aware that your cybersecurity insurance policy (if you have one) can help get you started. A good cybersecurity insurance policy should be a separate policy from your E & O insurance, as it will be more comprehensive and will require most, if not all, of the cybersecurity services we have mentioned. Remote worker security is not hard, it can be done, and recent times have proven it. Due to COVID, working remotely will continue to increase all around the world. More employers are embracing flexible schedules for their remote teams, leading to new remote work trends and remote work options. Now it is time to implement the necessary security tools too!

The hard part is knowing and acknowledging that cybersecurity is a requirement, not a luxury; it is hard to implement and maintain, and it costs more than we want. Things have changed.

About the Author

Troy Solis, founder and President of SOL-I.S. Technology Solutions, started his career in technology as a radar and radio electronics technician in the US Navy. After eight years of service, he joined the medical device industry, where his talent for technology advanced him from electronics technician to roles in IT management and consulting. After a decade in staff positions, while consulting as a side business, he launched SOL-I.S. Technology Solutions in 2009. The company started as an IT Managed Services Provider (MSP) and then pivoted the service offerings to Cybersecurity Solutions Provider in 2019.

Visit our website at www.sol-is.com, and to inquire about a cybersecurity assessment, submit your contact information at www.sol-is.com/contact.

Contact Troy Solis at:

Website: www.sol-is.com

Email: book@sol-is.com

Phone: (952) 279-2424

Facebook: gosolisgo

LinkedIn: sol-information-systems-llc

Twitter: solinfosystems

Practical Cybersecurity Tactics to Protect Your Business from Hackers

By Woodrow Cannon

I recently received a call from a prospective client on a normal Monday. They came into work that morning to find all of their files were encrypted and inaccessible. They had been hacked. Notices were posted in every folder about communicating with the hackers through email on how to get their files back. After days of downtime and intense negotiation, the hackers played hardball and the company had to pay Russian thugs a large sum of money in order to recover their crucial data. This wasn't a multi-million-dollar corporation. This was a small company just trying to survive in today's business climate. This exact scenario is playing out all over the world to companies both large and small every single day.

COVID changed how we all do business. In 2019, as employees started working from home more, companies had to change their networks to make data more accessible. Regrettably, more access to home users means more access for everyone. The above-mentioned company had no discernable antivirus, very little back-up, no spam filter, and their firewall was designed for home use rather than for business. In essence, they had been sitting ducks, and after such an attack, it was too late.

The burning question is: what can the average company do to protect itself?

That's where I come in. I initially started Thought Streams after switching jobs regularly after college. I would start a new job, fix their network, run out of tasks, get bored, and move on. After doing this for several years, I realized that if networks were set up correctly from the start, they could operate very efficiently and would only need light maintenance. Of course, that was in 2001, and times have changed.

These days, all networks (yes, even yours) are now under attack, 24/7. They need to be actively defended. Most companies that come to see me are small to mid-sized, and more often than not, they've grown organically, buying systems on Amazon or at Office Depot whenever they're needed. Generally, their IT has become a headache rather than an asset, and they need help turning that around. So here's some practical advice on setting your company up for solid security and peak performance.

Firewall

Your firewall is the main component of the internet side of your company. Every piece of crucial information is filtered through this device. It sits on the terrifying side of the internet. For this, you need a solid piece of equipment. <u>DO YOUR RESEARCH</u>. Most devices now are component-based. They will do content filtering, geographic filtering, and many other types of filtering, but generally require a yearly subscription. These components are there to protect your data, and I highly recommend using them. Not only do they protect, but they cut down additional traffic on your network, preserving your bandwidth. In the small office sphere, I like the Sophos XGS 87 and the XGS 116, but comparable devices can certainly work. All reputable firewalls need regular updates, so these are not just devices to put in place and ignore. Firmware updates are crucial to these devices and must be applied regularly. Firmware is the software that the firewall uses to boot and operate and can become out of date quickly, sometimes making them vulnerable to attack. Monitoring logs for attacks and odd traffic is a must, as this device will generally be the first device to show when you've been breached.

Anti-Spam and Email Domain Configuration

One of the main points of network intrusion is through email. Phishing refers to those emails that appear to be legitimate but instead, attempt to trick you into entering your credentials on a false website. Phishing attacks are common and in this particular case, the "phish" they're trying to catch is you. This, combined with weaker security, is all hackers will need to compromise everything on your system. Getting a front-end spam filter to protect your network is a necessity. Microsoft's general spam filter is easily bypassed, and you'll want to have the ability to whitelist and blacklist addresses. Mailprotector and Proof Point are currently very good filters, but this can change with time. If a filter becomes less effective, you will want the ability to change. In addition, you will want to be sure to set up your domain with SPF (Sender Policy Framework) and DMARC (Domain-based Message Authentication, Reporting, and Conformance) records to prevent the spoofing of email on your own domain. These methods authenticate emails coming from your domain and limit spammers from pretending to send a real email to your company. I would also be cautious about publicizing user email addresses on your website and other locations. By giving hackers your email address and job function, you're giving them crucial data they didn't have before, and they've already gotten halfway to your username/password combination.

Antivirus

Antivirus has gone through many different phases over the years. It used to be that a simple antivirus was fine because by the time viruses made it to you, the antivirus was updated, and it could protect you. Now the effectiveness of antiviruses is lagging behind the ingenuity of virus creators, and it is exceedingly difficult to find an effective antivirus. There has been a big push into Next-Generation Antivirus packages, as most of you that have received your Cybersecurity Insurance Policy renewal have seen. These Next-Gen packages do a very good job of not only finding threats based on behavior but also protecting the data and setup that you have. Currently, SentinelOne is my favorite, but again, this may change over time.

As Antivirus companies grow and develop, there may be better ones that overtake Sentinel. It's always good to listen and ask what others are using.

Training and Social Hacking

An informed user is a safer user. Running phishing simulations on your users (and making them aware you are running them) can be a very effective way of training your employees on how to identify suspicious emails and protect their private information. Implementing email campaigns and videos to keep users engaged and aware of the dangers is also very helpful.

Users need to be cautious of people that call on the phone and ask for passwords, no matter who they claim to be. Phone numbers are publicized on websites, and hackers have gotten very good at spoofing phone numbers and pretending to be from IT, an employer, or almost anyone in authority. They are very skilled at gleaning information from an unsuspecting user.

Privatizing your social media is helpful too. Many users have their name and email address listed on a company website as the company owner, manager, or accountant. From there, it can be an easy task to hop onto LinkedIn, Facebook, Instagram, Twitter, or future social media sites and pull a spouse's name, a child's name, dates of birth, and a virtual treasure trove of other information. This can be used to guess passwords and create more personal phishing or wire transfer emails. I am well aware this will decrease the number of possible views/likes/shares on social media, but it's an easy fix for an enormous problem.

Deep fakes are also becoming more and more popular. The filters most people use to adjust their faces and voices can also be used for more nefarious purposes, such as asking for passwords and convincing users to make financial transactions. As stated earlier, COVID and the ease of working from home have made it very common to make these requests over email. Your users have to be aware that it is a good practice to double-check any uncommon requests.

We are also hearing of hacking groups actively offering money for credentials. A Tesla employee was offered $1 million for administrator credentials for their network.[15]

This is the very scary side of social hacking. If a disgruntled employee hears two other people saying the administrator password, you need to be prepared to defend against an attack from someone that knows your password.

SOC/SEIM

Here we solve another big networking issue. Business networks are under attack 24/7, but most users and their IT counterparts are only available 40 (or most likely, 60) or so hours a week. It's important to have your network monitored during downtime. A SOC (Security Operations Center) and SEIM (Security Information and Event Management) fill the gap in monitoring. Essentially your company shares a Security Operations Center with other companies. A team of network professionals will monitor your network and email full-time and apply a preset fix to conditions that arise. They can take machines off the network, block IP addresses, and block access to an email box under a specific set of conditions. It also allows your IT professionals the ability to sleep without worrying about the security of your network.

Firmware and Software Updates

Firmware and Software updates are one of the most important tools available to you, and one of the most time-sensitive. By the time software or hardware has become compromised, it's very likely under active attack on the web. Firewalls, due to their nature, are one of the most susceptible to attack. Firewall updates need to be applied very quickly, generally as soon as available in the case of security updates.

Windows Servers also need this kind of constant maintenance. Each week provides another set of Windows updates that need to be checked and applied. I know that sometimes these updates bring with them a whole new set of problems, but these are generally much better than allowing hackers the ability to elevate their unprivileged account to an administrator account due to a bug. Microsoft recently had high profile vulnerabilities in both Exchange Server and their print functionality that allowed this kind of access.[16] Patches needed to be applied immediately, and in the case of Exchange, moving off the platform entirely was recommended.[17]

Workstations also need to be regularly patched and need to run an operating system that isn't end-of-life.

Microsoft will deem older operating systems end-of-life and will no longer provide any sort of patches for them once they are on that list. For Microsoft workstations, this means updating at least to Windows 10 or 11. Earlier versions are no longer patched and are very vulnerable right now. Sometimes special circumstances require older workstations and servers to stay online, but there are ways to mitigate their threat, such as separating them from the rest of the network or keeping them offline entirely.

Multi-Factor Authentication

This is one of the easiest ways to secure your network, but also one of the most maligned. Multi-factor authentication essentially gives you a second way of verifying your identity outside of your username and password. Generally, this involves a follow-up challenge after your username and password and will ask for a code or some sort of confirmation from your smartphone. (There are other variants of multifactor authentication, but this is the most common.) The main drawbacks to multi-factor authentication are the speed of login, and the need to have your phone handy when you are logging in. However, this is one of the best ways to combat hackers. There are, of course, ways to bypass the authentication, but generally, this involves a social element rather than a technical one. Hackers will generally try to trick the user into giving out their code either through email, text, or phone calls.

I highly recommend setting up multi-factor authentication wherever it is offered. If you have a mission-critical online tool that doesn't support MFA, I recommend you ask the provider to implement it. The time it costs is well worth the security it provides.

Active Monitoring

This one is the one that requires the most work of them all. Pay attention to your network on the whole. Generally, hackers that gain access to a network spend 11 days on the network before they are noticed.[18] Watch for unusual things such as strange applications showing up on your systems; new user accounts (especially ones with elevated privileges); strange behavior on your servers or the network; and even odd reboots or mouse movements.

There are monitoring tools that can watch out for this as well and can notify you if some of the above happen. Overall, just using good sense is helpful.

Backups

I list this last for a reason. It's not that backups aren't important. They are VITALLY important. However, once your network is recovered from a backup, you've already failed to protect it. Ransomware gangs will spend the days they exist on your network stealing whatever data they can get their hands on — employee records, customer data, credit card information, social security information, email addresses, etc. Anything that can be used against you.

Unfortunately, even if you recover through backups, they can still extort money from your company. Back-ups can only be considered the last line of defense because they're not really a defense, they are disaster recovery. The disaster has already happened.

I know this is a lot to think about. I often get asked, "Which of the above 9 steps is the most important to protect your data?" The simple answer is, all of them. I know it's a costly endeavor, but this kind of layered approach to defense is needed because the different vectors of attacks are as variable as the number of digital terrorists out on the web. We are all waging a war and, right now, the terrorists are winning. Every day new styles of attack are born. Your defense must be as adaptable and varied as the attackers'.

There's a reason in medieval times they didn't build a moat around half of the castle.

Build the whole moat. Protect yourself. Let me know if you need help.

About the Author

Woodrow Cannon is a computer extraordinaire. He grew up with computers and was programming from the age of 8 and just understands how they operate. After graduating from a fledgling IT program at the University of Alabama in 1994, he worked in the field from 1994 to 2001.

He started Thought Streams, Inc. in 2001 in an effort to better utilize his knowledge. Since then, he has helped countless companies maximize performance and improve security through more robust and efficient IT networking. Over the years he has been at the forefront of a rapidly expanding computer world. Recently he saw the necessity of enhanced cybersecurity and changed the focus of Thought Streams to include this growing need in an internet-connected world.

These days he spends his time much like Superman. By day he defends the weak and weary against the evils of cyber shenanigans. By night, he reads sci-fi novels to his 2 daughters and often enjoys a cocktail on the porch with his wife and neighbors. Instead of leaping tall buildings, he hurdles Legos and dog toys.

He lives outside of Atlanta in Peachtree City, Georgia, and can be reached at wcannon@thoughtstreams.com or on the web at http://book.yourtech.co.

Contact Woodrow Cannon at:

Website: https://www.thoughtstreams.com

Email: wcannon@thoughtstreams.com

Phone: 770.742.2688

LinkedIn: https://www.linkedin.com/in/woodrow-cannon-5a52232/

How Your Business Weaknesses Are a Hacker's Playground

By Tom Woolley

The online age has given rise to an exciting explosion of eCommerce opportunities. Traditional businesses are suddenly growing across physical boundaries and reaching customers never before accessible in their own backyards. And for that reason, there are more entrepreneurs entering the market on a daily basis than ever before in history.

Cheap technology, fast internet, and billions of connected potential customers have created a rapidly growing entrepreneurial playground where virtual service delivery allows us to work together across vast distances like we're sitting in the same office. You can connect with your accountant, talk with a vendor and interview a new employee all without ever getting in your car.

But like any playground, everyone is going to want to play whether they're invited or not. Tearing down the brick-and-mortar walls of old offices comes with some pretty big risks. Not just for us, but for our customers. The move to virtual often also means invisible. Securing the paperwork or sensitive information we collect about our clients is no longer as easy as locking a file cabinet or securing the doors.

In fact, the same virtual environment that so readily connects us to our business can lead to disaster. Companies are vulnerable to cyber-attacks because the same technology that connects them to their business from anywhere in the world also connects cybercriminals.

Companies of all sizes have to become proactive about preventing an attack because hackers are always looking for an opportunity to exploit a weakness in cybersecurity. It's at that point we start to realize that like many playgrounds, this one has a bully.

At this point, you might be thinking, "I've been on the internet for years and it's never been a problem."

While hacking is nothing new, things have changed. Cyber-attacks are up and there's a lot of value in user information. According to the IRS, 33% of citizens in the US have experienced identity theft. The FTS cataloged 2.2 million cases just in 2022, a substantial increase from prior years. And that's just identity theft.

Hackers could employ any number of digital weapons, such as Trojans, botnets, malware, distributed denial-of-service (DDoS) attacks, email scams (phishing), and even text messaging scams. Once the target of their attention, the harassment can be relentless and brutal with infected systems causing expensive and disastrous damage to your business.

With that in mind, there are 9 weaknesses that hacker playground bully is going to try to exploit.

Unprotected Computers

It costs a lot more time and money to lose data than to prevent it. Advanced cybersecurity software will provide basic protection against online threats on a software level only such as antivirus and malware. However, many small business owners are too busy running their business, so ensuring that the free trial that came with an employee's computer was extended, is rarely a priority.

When given an option, employees will often choose lower security settings for convenience, offering less protection. Relaxing the firewall, not encrypting the hard drive, and doing fewer updates are all methods that hackers rely on for sneaking their software onto business systems.

Lack of Training & Monitoring

Cybersecurity can be challenging for smaller business-es, often limiting their budget for support and training. An in-house team of cybersecurity experts is very expensive with even the best companies struggling to recruit top talent.

This lack of resources presents hackers with the oppor-tunity to exploit systems that haven't been properly configured to prevent them from stealing sensitive information. It also means employees and processes are not always trained on the latest threats or the need to consider how their actions can affect the company and its customers.

Something as innocent as copying a file folder into a different directory could cause the folder to be accidentally shared across the entire internet. As was the case when a university staff member copied a folder containing all students' loan information into a folder, they didn't realize was shared on the computer network.

Missing Online Safety Policies

In 2022, every business needs a cybersecurity policy. Your written policy should outline standards for securely accessing the internet, shielding employees from possible dangers and exploits, protecting the company from liabilities, and ensuring all customers have a safe and secure experience.

Doing business online means your customers are expecting their data to be handled responsibly. The company must provide a secure environment for conducting transactions and protect sensitive private information from hackers looking to commit identity theft or financial fraud.

Threats can also come from inside the company. Former and current employees, competitors, and business partners who are aware of a lack of monitoring or detection methods can easily take sensitive and valuable information. Establishing rules on how employees use company devices, passwords, share data, or even information over social media and websites can make a big impact on reducing your chances of being a victim.

Not Protecting Stored Data and Employee Information

Social engineering is one of the hackers' most sinister methods to exploit your business weaknesses. People are busier than ever and often juggling multiple communication channels at once. Hackers take advantage of the situation by using publicly available information to manipulate employees, customers, or even vendors into sharing confidential information. Every piece of public information shared online has the potential to be used against you.

Unsecured data is an open invitation for hackers to enter the sandbox and take advantage. When using cloud storage services such as Google Drive or Microsoft OneDrive, many business owners assume security is an automatic feature. However, it's actually the opposite. Cloud drives are almost always protected by a simple password that can be reset via email.

You might also be surprised to learn that most cloud storage providers do not back up your data. They often provide a restore function for bringing files back from the trash can. This is why emptying the trash can is the first thing a hacker will do after deleting your valuable information. It's always nice when someone else takes out the trash. But not in this case!

Not Encrypting Data Sent Online

Sending files online is a common security weakness and is a great opportunity for cybercriminals to intercept sensitive data. Business owners and employees often forget how much sensitive information can be readily available on a single document. You must encrypt it first or use a cloud service that offers end-to-end data encryption.

Professionals such as CPAs, tax accountants, and attorneys are particularly at risk for having sensitive non-encrypted data. It's difficult to prevent a client from unintentionally sending their own sensitive information across the internet without protecting it. Something as innocent as a tax return emailed to an employee can open up the entire company to liability. That document could sit in the employee's email inbox or archive for months or years without the business owner's knowledge.

Any hacker who gains access to a company email account would have access to what has become a historical treasure chest of documents. If those documents are encrypted, the risk is at least mitigated, and the company has not breached its responsibility to protect clients. However, if the client sent unprotected information and the company leaves it there, then it has assumed all future liability for owning unprotected client information.

Customers should be trained to share information via secure methods only. Placing reminders in unsecured messaging channels such as Facebook messenger or text messaging that customers may still have access to is a great way to avoid risk. It also helps reinforce the use of a secure method of sending files such as encrypted website upload buttons and encrypted email ensuring files are end-to-end encrypted and safe.

Even with the best training, accidents can happen. Businesses can proactively protect themselves with email server software that scans and detects infected files, unencrypted documents, or even messages that contain sensitive data such as social security or bank account numbers. Those messages can be automatically rejected before ever creating a security problem.

Lack of Online Safety Culture

Creating a security-first culture, by training employees and new customers to always question if the data they're sharing is sensitive, is a critical first step to closing this weakness. The switch to remote working in recent years has exposed many non-tech-savvy employees to online threats. It's also opened companies up to increased cyber-attacks.

The convenience of technology anywhere and everywhere also introduces the burden of being aware of what situations create weaknesses that hackers prey on. Hybrid working situations where files are accessed in-office and from home make it more difficult to be mindful of the risks when using connections such as unsecured public Wi-Fi in an airport. Employees need to be trained to transfer information securely and prevent unauthorized access to company networks, notice dangerous websites or fall for online scams.

Data theft has become a multi-billion-dollar industry. The days of broken grammar, bad spelling, and scammy subject lines are coming to an end. Online criminals have become incentivized to create more sophisticated methods. Phishing scams, where cybercriminals pretend to be legitimate vendors or customers to obtain personal information from employees, have become more common. In many cases, they will use data from breached email accounts to study and design a much more convincing scam email.

Management must encourage a workplace culture that understands how important cybersecurity is to protect business customers and reputation. There should be an established cyber incident response team with a plan that empowers employees to handle potential breaches, provides a method for reporting potential threats, and includes ongoing training.

Most importantly, employees should be encouraged to constantly question before sending personal or sensitive information, especially if the request sounds or feels suspicious. Messages coming through unfamiliar channels, such as your boss suddenly texting you or a customer reaching out via Facebook Messenger when they typically don't use those methods of communication should be confirmed by reaching out via a phone call where you can hear their voice.

Not Requiring Complex Passwords and 2-Factor Authentication

When asked how many logins they have to remember, most business owners and employees list the top 10 to 12 they use the most. However, most businesses have dozens of software systems they use to run their businesses. When you add in the accounts that exist but are not often used such as Adobe Acrobat, the number of logins and passwords easily tops one hundred.

Without a password solution such as a password vault, single sign-on, or identity management system, employees will often write down passwords, or worse, they'll store them in a spreadsheet or text file right on their computer. You would be surprised how many employees keep a text file on their Windows desktop titled "Passwords" so they can remember and track the large number of usernames and passwords they use on a monthly basis.

Every employee should create strong passwords consisting of numbers, letters, and special characters and be twelve to sixteen characters long. Password vaults and login management systems will allow employees to easily generate random passwords while storing them in the vault under a master password. Using a randomly generated password with that kind of criteria makes guessing a password impossible.

The master password should have the same requirements but can be something more easily memorized.

Protecting the master password is very important! Discovering that password does make any hacker 'King of Playground,' so pairing it with 2-factor authentication (2FA) ensures your password vault is much more secure.

Enabling 2FA is a common source of frustration for businesses. The most common methods of setting up 2FA include an authenticator app on the employee's phone or a code sent via text or email with a short expiration time. Requiring that code makes it almost impossible for a cybercriminal to breach that account, even if they have a working username and password. Many companies lacking dedicated technical support staff can find the task of enabling and training employees on 2FA daunting and ultimately decide to never enforce it. But having that cybersecurity-centric culture also means encouraging employees to accept the minor inconvenience of having that extra code versus the major headache and expense of going through a security breach.

Reviewing Cyber Protections as Systems Evolve

As the business grows, its technology needs and requirements evolve along with it. Signing up for new software such as video conferencing, project management or remote collaboration all add significant operational advantages to help employees do their jobs more effectively and efficiently. It also introduces new methods of attack for a cybercriminal looking for new weaknesses in a previously secure environment.

Waiting for an attack to occur to determine if security protocols are still working and cover all vulnerabilities is just asking for disaster. Reviewing cybersecurity policies quarterly, and checking servers, cloud applications, storage, and servers, will ensure your business is fully secured as it changes.

Backup systems can unexpectedly stop working over time. Verifying backup systems by checking that files are present and recent. It's also important to try opening them and attempting to restore a few files. The worst time to find backup systems stopped working or are creating corrupt files is when a hacker has already stolen your files and deleted them from your own storage.

It's also a great idea to keep track of assets that already have data on them to make sure they're still there. This may sound a bit weird, but a major business weakness is tracking where data may have been stored and forgotten. Common culprits are old computers that have been replaced and tossed in a closet to be forgotten. Backups also take up a lot of space and may be copied to longer-term storage such as physical discs or cheaper online storage locations. Those files still contain your company and customers' critical personal information and should be checked on a regular basis.

Having a clutter bug or hoarder managing the data systems can be just the thing a cybercriminal needs to cash in on critical and private information. If that old computer is never coming back into service, it's a great time to go ahead and securely delete all information on the hard drive using a file erasing tool that will ensure no residual data exists on the drive for a hacker to restore.

Businesses also tend to keep too many backups. In the event of a security breach, employees aren't going to be searching for a copy of a file they were working on 6 months ago. They're going to want to get the most recent copy, so 4 to 6 weeks of the most recently altered files is really all that needs to be stored. By minimizing the amount of data a company is stockpiling, they're reducing their vulnerability to loss.

Proactively Scanning and Monitoring Networks for Breaches

Without establishing a process, policy, and responsible party there are critical tasks that weaken every company's cyber defenses. Older software and devices that aren't able to be updated anymore create an easily targetable weakness. Those devices may contain software with security vulnerabilities that aren't being patched anymore and are secretly lurking around waiting to be exploited.

User-friendly browsers often try to make life easier by helping remember the passwords to log into frequently used sites. Purging those old usernames and passwords from the software on a regular basis helps to prevent former employees or someone who obtains a lost or stolen computer from accessing or deleting the company's valuable data.

Hackers can also use external drives such as USB thumb drives or external hard drives to slip malicious software onto business systems and bypass external defenses. Drives received through the mail, from other users, or even from conferences should be assumed to be dangerous until thoroughly scanned by enterprise-grade endpoint protection software.

While it may be tempting to pick up a computer from the local technology retailer or order it online, those systems aren't designed to protect your business or its information right out of the box. These computers guide the user into creating a local administrator account with all privileges. That means a hacker, virus, malware, or ransomware that finds its way into that machine will also have the same unrestricted access.

New employees who receive their first company computer should always receive a system that is configured into the company's security policies first. Setting the user to a restricted account ensures the employee has all the necessary access needed to do their job without restriction. It also means they can't install software or access unsecured websites without authorization to avoid harmful third-party websites or apps from installing viruses that could unknowingly compromise the entire system.

The lucrative nature of cybercrime makes preventing cyber-attacks crucial for every business's survival. It takes a lot of effort, time, and money to recover from a breach incident and will involve working with local law enforcement authorities to resolve it. Business activities likely come to a painful halt while forensic auditors determine the cause of the breach and set up new systems to detect and prevent future threats.

Taking measures to secure data, train employees, and create cybersecurity policies may seem like a daunting or low-priority task. However, businesses that lose customer data or fail to report a loss are guaranteed to suffer damage to their reputation. Those that are in relationship businesses built on trust such as financial, legal, and medical professions are often unable to recover from the sudden loss of business and close their practice or spend years recovering what was lost.

About the Author

Tom Woolley is a tech-obsessed accountant gone serial entrepreneur. After graduating with his MBA in Accounting from Columbia and over 15 years in corporate finance technology for pharmaceuticals and oil and gas, Tom established Today CFO during the early days of the cloud accounting trend.

In 2019, Today CFO made a dramatic shift from working entirely in the traditional office environment to working remotely which presented a new set of unique challenges. Securing client data while allowing employees to work remotely is a huge challenge for the financial industry.

Finding and implementing the right solution for his own firm and clients revealed a huge gap in expectation versus reality for accounting firm owners. What started as an immediate critical need quickly became an obsession that ignited a passion for internet security that led to the creation of Today Cybersecurity. A firm established with the mission of securing online financial firms and their clients from online predators with the right technology and training without the need for massive enterprise infrastructure or expensive IT staff.

Tom now spends his time spreading awareness on how important cybersecurity is to protect your firm and client data from falling into hackers' hands as well as how firms can reduce costs while meeting their legal obligations. They also focus on why skipping due diligence can result in a cyber-attack that destroys your reputation and causes over 90% of firms to close their doors in less than 3 months.

Contact Tom Woolley at:

Website: https://www.todaycybersecurity.com/

Email: tom@todaycybersecurity.com

Phone: 832-334-2426

LinkedIn: https://www.linkedin.com/in/tom-woolley-0b72651ab

5 Cybersecurity Strategies for Service-Based Businesses

By Ross Dahman

Question: starting today, how are you addressing cybersecurity risks in your organization?

Confronting life's challenges and uncertainties, comes down to a **tradeoff** between **being pro-active** vs **being reactive** in addressing risks of all kinds and certainly cybersecurity risks.

As Chris Krebs, the first and former Director of CISA, notes below, a cyber-attack is a **WHEN** proposition— not an **IF** proposition—your day, my day, and everyone's day—the "**BOOM**" is-a-coming. As Chris comments: just how prepared are you to contain the blast radius?

As this table below illustrates, by objectively examining your organization, bottom-up, in the calm and clarity of the pre-attack environment, which is **LEFT of BOOM**, and then taking concrete, corrective and affirmative protective pro-active measures, which while not easy, nor quick, requiring single-mindedness and diligence, puts you miles down the road when the day of the attack occurs—the **BOOM**—and in confronting the subsequent aftermath, **RIGHT of BOOM**.

Your Options	Questions?	Answers!
Are you choosing to start on the solid footing of the Pro-active path?	How? By asking the **hard** and **confrontative** questions upfront!	This Pro-active path leads to **easy** answers further down the path: having the resources and preparation done, ready to go **when** you will most certainly be needing them!
Or, are you choosing to start on the slippery slope of the Re-active path?	How? By **NOT** asking the **hard** and **confrontative** questions upfront!	This Re-active path leads to **hard** answers further down the path: by **NOT** having the resources and preparation done, ready to go **when** you will critically need them, puts you in a scrambling, weakened, exposed and precarious posture!

No one is able to prevent a cyber-attack—not even the United States Government!

Recently, I was in Chicago and saw this Chicago Police patrol car:

The Chicago Police Department is implicitly stating: we are here to **serve and protect**—**not serve and prevent** any and every possible misfortune that might come your way!

Said another way by **Benjamin Franklin**: an ounce of prevention (i.e., protection) is worth a pound of cure.

What does this mean?

As one of the Founding Fathers of the United States, he was stating emphatically that it is far better to take stringent protective or preventative measures now— i.e., pro-actively, *we start doing what is necessary today*—rather than to suffer severe consequences later —i.e., defensively reacting to a cyber breach, which may take months, or years, to fully recover from and your organization will probably never be the same!

Robert Burton said it another way: *penny wise, pound foolish*—this is a recipe for upset and calamity!

If you know better, then please: do better!

For service organizations, creating a cybersecurity capability in your organization involves three key components:

1. People
2. Processes
3. Technology or Tools

While all are important, **people** are the key: being both a resource and constraint, they have the most conse-quential impact on your organization. People are signif-icantly engaged with both **processes** and **technology** in your organization—they need your guidance and leadership!

Therefore, let's first focus on a **people-centric approach**: how are your people able to drive cybersecurity aware-ness and instill best cyber practices throughout your organization?

The most important component is **education**:

- First: train your people to understand what are the different types of cybersecurity attacks.

- Second: inform them of actions they can take to pro-actively mitigate against the likelihood of an attack being successful.

- Third: provide your people, with a checklist (please email info@huntleigh.com, with cybersecurity checklist in the subject line, for a copy of this checklist), when attacked, as to whom does what, where and when?

ONE: Building an organizational culture of cybersecurity FIRST

Building an **organizational culture** of cybersecurity first will pay long-term dividends.

What is meant by an **organizational culture** of cyber-security first?

Educate your team that we live in a world today of 24/7/365 round-the-clock ongoing and continuous cyber-attack attempts—these attacks probably will never stop!

Cyber-attackers are attempting to steal your money, and your data, embarrass and harm you, and make your life absolutely miserable!

Whatever it takes for a cyber-attacker to be successful, they will figure out a way to do so—they do not give a flip about you!

So, please include all of your staff, so that they feel engaged, invested and appreciated—this goes a long way and will pay you big dividends! Consider having one-on-one's with each member, to let them know that they are the organization's front line of defense against cyber-attacks, both online or at the organization's physical locations. They should be informed that a cyber-attack not only puts your organization in jeopardy but their jobs as well. Emphasize that constant vigilance is a necessity and speaking up counts: ***if you see something, say something!***

With guidance and support—and ongoing gentle reminders, with frequent mini-educational cyber lessons—your team becomes a **force multiplier** against cyber-attacks. Without it, your organization becomes low hanging fruit for the bad guys to rip off: which do you prefer?

TWO: Social Engineering, also known as Phishing Detection Training

Phishing attacks are aimed every day at each of your team members—no one is immune—all are being targeted! Such attacks may be significantly mitigated through the use of specialized tools, such as **spam filters** and **business email compromise (BCE)** platforms:

- **Spam filters:** block obnoxious or unsolicited emails.

- **BCE:** in-flight captures suspicious or malicious emails.

- **Both:** are vitally needed!

Each organization is a separate "tenant" in a BCE platform and is, therefore, regarded as a unique entity by BCE's Artificial Intelligence engine. The AI engine develops ongoing and updated specific email signature profiles for each tenant, based on the organization's email history and end-user behavior by the organization's people.

Accordingly, an email may be classified by the BCE platform as:

1. **Low/no risk:** passed through without delay

2. **Medium risk:** the email is pulled aside, which gives discretion to the end-user as to whether or not to accept or reject the email

3. **High risk:** the email is quarantined automatically

THREE: Access Management

An organization's lifeblood is its data and its control over this data. **Privileged Access Management (PAM)** is a gating tool, driven by a Rules Engine, which protects valuable data by enforcing and permitting:

1. Who has access to what data?

2. To what level of access—i.e., how privileged—is each staff member as to what levels they are allowed to access the data?

3. How many minutes, per session, and over a defined period of time, including the number of aggregated minutes, is the user granted access to the data?

4. What day(s) and time of day are users permitted to access the data?

Consider implementing a policy of **Zero Trust**: this assumes that no user has an inherent right to access any organizational data. Access to all data sets must be vetted on a per-user and per-data set basis. **Password management** is foundational for **Privileged Access Management (PAM).**

Passwords are the keys that open the doors to many organizational kingdoms: operating systems, stored data, online apps, being authorized to conduct financial transactions, view streaming events, etc.

Using **password management tools** will promote and support good password hygiene:

1. A different password is required for each account

2. Good passwords are combinations of alpha-numeric-special characters—the resulting

password must be easy to use and incredibly difficult to guess

3. No sharing of passwords—every staff member uses only their own passwords and no one else's passwords.

4. Periodic changing up of passwords: stolen passwords are trafficked on the dark web—by frequently changing passwords, you will render worthless any previously filched passwords.

FOUR: Identity Management

Multi-Factor Authentication (MFA) is a must—an absolute prerequisite—to authenticate that a user is actually that user!

An organization must have at least two (2) forms of user authentication—this is a bare minimum!

However, having three (3) forms of user authentication is much better!

Password Authentication Hierarchy:

1. **First-level authentication**: passwords them-selves are a first form of authentication.

2. **Second-level authentication**: might be use of an Authenticator, like those provided by Microsoft or Google; providing a six-to-nine numeric code,

which is sent as SMS text message to the user's smartphone or email address.

3. **Third-level authentication**: a security token/fob might be provided by a third party like a RSA token, which may be physical or virtual.

4. **Alternative Third-level or Fourth-level authentication**: Biometric security might be added as an additional form of authentication: fingerprint scan, iris scan, facial recognition.

FIVE: Protecting Critical Data

The best way to protect your data is to have it **backed-up,** on a scheduled basis, to a secure offsite location. However, backed-up data is only as good as your ability to restore your data, in a predictable manner and on a timely basis. Further, in the event of an attack, knowing the **prioritization** of what data is restored first, then second, etc., will minimize the impact of an attack.

This is the value of doing Table Top exercises, including Penetration (PEN) Testing.

Table Top exercises are practice fire drills, done beforehand—when there is minimal stress and little anxiety; so, when there is a real fire, with heightened stress and punishing anxiety, a focused, fast and effective response is a realistic possibility.

Why is an effective response possible?

Because you will have done the heavy lifting by going through rigorous fire drills, including **Table Top exercises** and **PEN testing,** beforehand, allowing you to move with clarity, confidence, and certainty in the right direction.

Wounded or MIA Data

However, even though your data is backed-up offsite, and your **Table Top exercises** and **PEN testing** has prepared you for a successful and rapid response, this does not prevent unauthorized day-to-day access to your data, or prevent data from being corrupted, or lost, before it is backed-up.

Privileged Access Management, Zero-Trust, and **Password Management** will go a long way toward data integrity. There are data management tools, which constantly monitor who is accessing your data, and what they are doing with it—are they downloading it to a USB thumb drive?

Similarly, there are network management tools, which monitor users on the network: what are they doing, are they attempting to access off-limit areas, like log files, or attempting to elevate their privileges, without proper authorization?

These users may be your people, your customers, your vendors, or cyber-attackers, who have gained unauthorized access to some or all of your network. They may be exploring how they are able to move laterally within your network, to probe for areas of weakness, which may be exploited.

FIVE: Cybersecurity Company Playbook.

When do you plant a shade tree? Answer: 20 years ago—or today!

Moral: best to plan ahead and start now!

Like your organization's operations and procedures handbook, it's most important to also have a cyber-security handbook or playbook: one for staff, one for managers, and one for executives. Ideally, these hand-books would be customized and developed for each department within your organization: accounting, finance, compliance, IT, operations, sales, marketing, etc.

To be valuable, these guidelines must be developed with initial input coming from a grassroots level, within your organization and then built upwards. This way the playbooks are grounded in reality, appropriately nuanced, and genuinely useful.

Included in these handbooks might be topics like an inventory of all data assets—who monitors and man-ages these assets, where are these assets located, how are they secured, who/how/when are they accessed? Further, when is the next technology refresh update for these assets and how/when/where is this done?

Further, to develop organizational robustness and resil-iency, start now to develop **data flow diagrams (DFD)** of operational workflows, within each department, across departments and outside the organization with customers and your supply chain vendors. Additionally, correlating operational workflows with **cash diagrams,** depicting the organization's cash workflows: how/when /where does **cash flow in** and how/when/where does **cash flow out?** Who/how is managing this cash workflow?

For playbooks and handbooks to stay relevant, they will need to be audited and updated on a scheduled basis, so playbooks and handbooks reflect today's policies, processes and procedures, not yesterday's policies, processes and procedures.

Final thoughts:

- "For small-medium sized organizations having an MSP is an ABSOLUTE MUST".

- "An attack is a WHEN proposition, not an IF proposition. You better figure out ahead of time how to limit the blast radius."

- "You can't catch all the arrows: better be prepared!"

Comments excerpted from **Christopher Krebs'** presentation at 7 Figure MSP Live! event, August 24, 2022, Charlotte, NC.

Mr. Krebs was the first Director of the Department of Homeland Security's Cybersecurity and Infrastructure Security Agency (CISA). He is currently a Chair of the CISO Advisory Board; Senior Newmark Fellow in Cybersecurity, The Aspen Institute; Advisory Board Member, SentinelOne; Resident Scholar, Center for Politics, University of Virginia; and Founding Partner, Krebs Stamos Group, LLC

Chris Krebs, left, and **Ross Dahman**, **President** of **Huntleigh Technology Group**, at 7 Figure MSP Live! event, August 24, 2022, Charlotte, NC.

About the Author

Ross Dahman is the President of Huntleigh Technology Group, 915-832-0100, which he founded in 1990. The company's origins began as a Telecommunications service provider and was the first Internet Service Provider in El Paso, TX in 1994, as well as one of the first ISPs in Texas. The company has entered into the MSP/MSSP space with a focus on cybersecurity.

Contact Ross Dahman at:

Website: www.huntleigh.com

Email: ross.dahman@huntleigh.com

Phone: 915-225 -2499

LinkedIn: https://www.linkedin.com/in/rossdahman/

Cyber-Criminal 101:
What Are They After
and How do I Protect Myself?

By Logan Edmonds

Imagine this: You're the financial secretary of a small non-profit organization located in a historic building in a major metropolitan area. You have a small team, of 6 to 8 people, and you have big dreams about positively impacting your local community. You want to use your resources to accomplish this, but feel a reworking of your historic space is necessary to meet your goals. With this in mind, you go ahead and contract an architecture firm to assist you with the design of the rework of your space.

The project kicks off with much fanfare and excitement! The architecture firm your non-profit has hired is doing quality work and there is an upbeat attitude amongst your entire team that great things are going to happen when the project is completed. The architect lets you know they will send you an invoice as project milestones are completed per the terms of your contract. As expected, you receive an email requesting the first installment of the project fee from the architecture firm. It's pricey, but the email address, letterhead of the invoice, and timing all check out. Plus, they are a great firm doing great work, so you pay it without a second thought by cutting a check.

All is well, and the project continues as usual. The following month you receive a second invoice from the firm. Again, it's a bit pricey, but all the details check out, so you cut another check. This scenario repeats again the next month, and again you pay. You've paid a lot of money at this point, over one hundred thousand dollars! A sense of something being off begins to develop. Do architects really cost this much for a project of this size? You haven't even paid the contractors for the construction yet!

After talking amongst your team, a consensus is reached that something is awry. You pick up the phone and call the architect's billing team. You send a copy of the invoices you received to the billing team and explain what has been going on, asking for clarification. The next words you hear make your stomach drops out from underneath you. The billing team of the architecture firm informs you that they have not yet sent an invoice yet, as the first milestone of the project is not yet completed.

How can this be? You ask them to check again, and their answer is still the same; no invoices have yet been sent out. You go back to the invoice emails and see something you had not noticed previously: the domain of the email address is one letter off from the actual website of the architecture firm. You have been scammed! Questions fly through your mind: Who would do this? How did they know so much about your non-profit and the architecture firm's relationship? After consulting with an IT company that you have worked with previously, it quickly becomes apparent that you are a victim of a cyber-criminal in what is commonly referred to as a "Business Email Compromise" or BEC attack.

Scary right? This was a scenario my company Tabernacle Technology Solutions had to step into when this client reached out to us for help. We specialize in assisting businesses and organizations in both being proactive regarding managing their cyber risk as well as helping them recover after an incident happened. This client was confused and uncertain of what their next steps should be. What do you do when such a large amount of money has been stolen from you and the police can't help?

Certain details above have been altered to help protect our client's identity, but here is a brief summarization of what we believe happened after forensics:

- The client's email environment was hacked by a cyber-criminal through one of many different methods (phishing, credential stuffing, brute-force password attacks, etc.)

- The criminal lurked in the environment for weeks before making a move. They were reading emails coming in and out of the non-profit and taking time to learn as much about them as possible. Once they understood the current situation, they acted by crafting a scam that uniquely made sense to this small-profit organization.

- They took the money almost immediately and moved it offshore. Out of over 6 figures in losses, my client recovered around $17,000 between the bank and their insurance policy. Most of the money never came back, even though they had an insurance policy for this kind of event. We still know very little about who the cyber-criminal was or where they were operating from.

Unfortunately, the above scenario is happening at a staggering frequency amongst small to medium-sized organizations right now. A cyber-criminal will spend sums of time ranging in the timelines of weeks or months targeting a specific small business or organization. I like to tell my clients that the image of a cyber-criminal being someone in a hoodie typing on a glowing keyboard in a dark room is an outdated cliché. Rather, it is often people in cubicles with headsets, laptops, and a whiteboard with a SWOT analysis of their targets written on it. Cybercrime is an official cottage industry, and it is growing at a break-neck pace.

To quote a classic line from Sun Tzu's *The Art of War*: "If you know the enemy and know yourself, you need not fear the result of a hundred battles. If you know yourself but not the enemy, for every victory gained you will also suffer a defeat. If you know neither the enemy nor yourself, you will succumb in every battle." Why would anyone do this? What is going through their mind as they systematically exploit small, medium, and large organizations? Why aren't they afraid of the consequences of law enforcement? These are all good questions! Let's do a brief analysis of the motivations of a cyber-criminal so we can learn more about what we are up against.

The first thing we need to admit is that cybercrime is not just a technology problem. This is also a people problem. Theft, scam artistry, exploitation, and apathy have all been a thing since time immemorial. Cyber-criminals are driven individuals with set goals in mind. For simplicity, we will break down cyber criminals into four separate categories: profit-driven criminals, nation-state-sponsored criminals, hacktivists, and insiders. However, it is important to note a single cyber-criminal can fall into multiple categories.

The profit-driven criminal: This is a cyber-criminal whose primary objective is illicit financial gain using technology as the primary vehicle to achieve this. Often, they will organize into gangs or groups to improve their efficiency and organization, just like a business. They treat everything in terms of how much money can they make at the expense of a business or organization they are targeting.

Ever heard of the Conti Ransomware gang? According to CNBC,[19] this is an existing group of cyber-criminals who specialize in ransomware: a form of cyber-attack that takes your business electronic data (Emails, documents, databases, etc.) makes it unreadable and then offers to give it back to you in exchange for a ransom payment. Conti operates just like a normal business, with a CEO, specialized positions like ransom negotiators, deal-closers, commissions for successful cyber-attacks, employee-of-the-month awards, and even an HR team for filling positions! With an estimated 350 employees and or contractors, they want to make money and are very successful at doing so. It is estimated that they have generated 2.7 billion dollars in successful ransom payments in the last 2 years!

The nation-state cyber-criminal: This is a cyber-criminal, either military or civilian, that is backed and protected from legal repercussions by a nation-state or world power. They are operating with the blessing of said power and operate with the intent to forward their sponsors' goals on the world stage. Conti, for example, is also suspected of being affiliated with the country of Russia by US Intelligence Officials and often works in tandem with Russian interests. According to the BBC[20], another example of this would be the Lazarus Group, which is likely backed by the North Korean government. One of their primary objectives appears to be financial theft through cybercrime worldwide in order to pad the heavily sanctioned nation-state's reserves. They are suspected of stealing at least four hundred million in financial and digital assets in 2021 alone!

The hacktivist: This is a group or individual that uses hacking to accomplish goals based on ideological or political goals. One of the most heavily publicized groups that would fall into this category is Anonymous, a loose group of technically inclined individuals famous for using hacking as a vehicle for expressing discontent related to political or ideological reasons. According to *The Guardian*,[21] when the Ukraine-Russian conflict erupted in early 2022, Anonymous declared war on Vladimir Putin and his administration. They took credit for disabling many government websites and Russia Today (a state-backed news publication), as well as hacking the Russian Ministry of Defense databases. Anonymous has also been tied to major domestic attacks according to *The Atlantic*.[22] This includes attacks that leaked internal polices files from over 200 agencies across the USA.

The Insider: As the name suggests, this is someone in a privileged position inside the organization or organizations that are targeted for a cyber-attack. This can be a disgruntled employee who wants to harm their employer or ex-employer in a significant manner. It can also be an employee or contractor who is bribed by an outside party to place malware or means of access within an organization. According to *Forbes*,[23] in 2019 a 34-year-old Pakistani man named Muhammad Fahd was extradited from Hong Kong to the U.S. for bribing AT&T employees. He was accused of paying as much as four hundred and twenty thousand dollars to a single AT&T staff member asking them to do things for him in exchange! This included unlocking phones from the AT&T carrier, installing malware on AT&T machines, or even just giving him their passwords so he could do the above actions himself. According to the US Department of Justice,[24] this scheme inflicted over two hundred million dollars in losses to AT&T Inc!

Why are these criminals not afraid of the consequences of law enforcement? There are a lot of factors in the answer to this question but let's start with a big one. According to the National Institute of Standards and Technology,[25] one of the primary factors to consider is that, unlike property crime, cybercrime requires no physical presence. Every company and organization has cyber assets (bank accounts, sensitive intellectual property, critical operational documentation, personally identifiable information, etc.) that can be stolen by cybercriminals without them ever having to leave their homes. This, combined with the fact a cyber-criminal can reach across international borders to commit the crime in question, creates a sticky law enforcement situation.

Consider this scenario: A Russian cyber-criminal perpetrates a cyber-attack on a US business with the intent of financial gain. How is US law enforcement supposed to arrest this individual even if they know who they are? Russia and the United States have no extradition treaty for criminals. This is not even considering the degree of anonymity the internet offers individuals in the first place. For example, how many users are on Twitter using a pseudonym instead of their real name? This rabbit hole goes deep, and due to various factors, cyber-criminals can often escape any kind of legal repercussions for their crimes.

How do we stop these cyber-criminals from attacking us? Unfortunately, with the success rate of cyber-criminals regarding cyber-attacks against businesses and organizations being so high, it is my opinion that the word "prevention" should be taken out of our vocabulary regarding cybersecurity. According to Fundera[26] There was a 424% increase in new small business cyber breaches in 2019 alone. The attackers simply have an overwhelming advantage. They know who we are, our addresses, phone numbers, email addresses, and more, thanks to the internet. On the other hand, often we can only guess who they are and what their motivations are.

Automation tools, which were supposed to be a great boon to making our lives easier, have been turned against us by cyber-criminals. They can use automation tools to cast a greater net, attacking more organizations than they could otherwise, as well as quickly identify the crown jewels of businesses (bank accounts, credit cards, Personal Identifiable Information, and more) once they have successfully broken into an organization. This combined with the extreme profitability of cyber-crime (*Cybercrime Magazine*[27] pegs the costs of cyber-crime for 2021 to be around 6 trillion dollars) means that the attackers are only going to escalate their efforts and grow as an industry.

How about us, the defenders? Can we automate this problem away in a similar manner that it is being weaponized against us? Automated programs are a great solution for routine tasks! They are a way to cut costs and address issues. Many problems in the modern world have been addressed using automated tools to great effect!

However, there is nothing routine about the task in front of us. These are flesh and blood humans targeting and working against us, not programs. They are launching sustained campaigns (often with timelines of weeks or months) against individual small businesses because even a small business of 5 employees can frequently net them a payday of high five figures. When pitted against human ingenuity, automation is frequently defeated. If your security program is completely automated, with no human eyes on it, common sense tells us it will eventually be defeated by the criminal. As an industry, we have been searching for the holy grail of completely automated security for nearly two decades now, to no avail. You can't buy a product that will fix this issue. This is one of the reasons cybersecurity professionals frequently state that attackers have the advantage in this fight. Tools can help, but they cannot fix this issue by themselves.

A great analogy for cybersecurity is the hull of a big ship at sea. Most large modern ships compartmentalize their hulls, sectioning the space off with barriers and compartments. This means should the hull be breached by an iceberg, only part of the ship will fill with water and the ship will still stay afloat. The 2018 standard of anti-virus software on all computers and multi-factor authentication are a great start, but they alone no longer compartmentalize the "hull" of your organization to the extent needed to keep it afloat during a major cyber-attack in 2022 forward.

Fundera sadly reports that 60% of small businesses that are victims of a cyber-attack go out of business within six months of the incident. Things have changed in recent years and doing things the same way we did them in 2018 is simply not sufficient to reduce the risk of cyber-crime to small and medium-sized organizations to where it needs to be. That's a rough equivalent of saying that it's ok for a semi-truck driver to be driving with twice the legal limit of alcohol in their blood since it is "close enough." The risk to us and others are still way too high to be acceptable.

Instead of "prevention," being the focus word for defenders the goal should be the word "protection." I get in my car every day knowing full well that driving to work can kill me. Why do I not lose sleep over this? Because between the car manufacturers' precautions and my own personal precautions, I believe I have reduced my risk to acceptable levels. I have not prevented the possibility of a car accident, but I have reduced my chances of complete catastrophe through protective measures both in my actions and the built-in safety features of my car.

A similar mindset should be applied to cybersecurity. If we cannot 100% prevent cyber-attackers from breaking in and causing damage, we should focus on reducing the ease with which they do and limiting the amount of damage they can cause in a single incident. This must be very intentionally and carefully done. There is a real demand for cybersecurity professionals in the United

States right now. *Cybercrime magazine*[28] predicts there will be 3.5 million openings in cybersecurity jobs in 2025. The demand is ever-growing and there are not enough people to fill the roles needed. So, what is the answer? There are only two realistic answers: Hire the necessary talent yourself in a very competitive job market, or partner with a Managed Security Service Provider (MSSP). For most small businesses and organizations, the latter makes more sense for a plethora of reasons.

A strategic partnership with an MSSP brings a host of benefits. First, let's start with security. You are partnering with a company whose sole focus is cybersecurity. They are seasoned in the areas of risk management and cybersecurity, providing similar services for a host of other businesses. They can serve all sorts of organizations and businesses in any market. For example, my company, Tabernacle Technology Solutions, is an MSSP that partners with organizations with as few employees as two and as many as five hundred plus. We have both non-profit organizations with under four-hundred thousand dollars a year in revenue, and businesses valued at a billion dollars partnering with us to make sure their cyber risk is being properly managed. We have curated a selection of tools, technologies, and expertise to best address the current cyber-risk climate. This is not an easy thing to do, requiring hundreds of hours of research and development.

Second, you are partnering with someone who is moving with the needs of your business at the forefront of their minds. An MSSP is more than just your IT guy, they are an advisor on the rapidly developing risk landscape that all businesses face. They advise you on the best strategies as you scale your business to meet the needs of the future and help you avoid the costly mistakes that a security misstep can cause you. A quality MSSP will be speaking with you at least quarterly for general strategy and to help you know how to stay safe and continue to grow in the modern landscape. You can visit our website https://tabernacle.tech, to learn more about what a quality MSSP should be offering.

About the Author

Logan Edmonds was born and currently lives in Columbus Ohio. With a passion for great customer service interactions and helping small businesses, Logan founded what was to become Tabernacle Technology Solutions in June of 2018. Logan specializes in advising small to medium-sized businesses on the best avenues and practices of managing their risk as it relates to proactively protecting their bottom line from cyber-attacks. In his personal time, Logan enjoys reading works of fiction and playing with his young daughter.

Contact Logan Edmonds, CEO & CRA at:

Website: https://tabernacle.tech

Email: information@tabernacle.tech

Phone: 614-412-2455

LinkedIn: https://www.linkedin.com/in/tabernaclecrs/

Why Your Business Needs to Implement a Cybersecurity Plan Now

By Matthew Jay

Tsunami.

Cybersecurity needs a word like Tsunami. A word that has an automatic, emotional, and widespread understanding. A word whose reputation has been defined, unfortunately, through extreme loss and devastation. We need that poster-child two-hundred-foot wave. Say "tsunami" to anyone in any language and it evokes vivid imagery. A wave with that magnitude glues itself inside our long-term memories; most of us have at least a vague idea of how tsunamis start, the geographies most at risk, the interest in monitoring, measuring, and alerting of these enormous waves, the alluring false comfort of the shore just before it approaches, not to mention the crippling aftermath left to the people and economy once the waters have receded.

The problem with cybersecurity is most threats never present themselves as a two-hundred-foot wall of water. Most cyber-attacks wax quietly into a network on average 120 days before anyone realizes it is even there. Disruption and devastation occur with little, or no warning. We are challenged as an industry because the Cyber Tsunami is a silent killer.

I'll wake up the silence later in this chapter, but for now, the only way to understand the tsunami is to dive headfirst into the cresting waves of today's cyber-threat landscape that's grown exponentially since 2021. The peek inside will scare you. It should. But as we push through the chapter, you will find confidence in the 3-Step Plan you can apply to your business. You might be up a creek, but at least you will have a paddle.

If you are a small business owner keeping this information at a comfortable arm's length, the bullet points below may press for a bit more intimacy. I'm not saying you must hug it, but a healthy vulnerability in accepting the vast problem in front of us would at least demonstrate you are invested in running a business past 2022. I'll start high, but then we'll end at ground zero and walk through the front door of your business. Small businesses, in general, are out-resourced and reside on the lower ground compared to larger corporations – never a good position in the shadow of a tsunami. Large corporations most certainly are not immune to cyber-attacks as they are high-value targets and attacks on these corporations are typically headline-worthy. But, don't let the headlines create a false sense of comfort for who is more frequently targeted: Small Businesses. Small businesses are low-hanging fruit. The statics ripen this case.

GLOBAL CYBER-DUNG

Let's start from the top, since the proverbial dung of cyber-warfare rolls downhill. Cyber-warfare is very real among nation-states. Russia, China, India, and the United States, to highlight a few – are all active parti- cipants sharpening their cyber-warfare tactics as a means of gaining leverage over the next. The fallout of these nation-state cyber-attacks creates waves of opportunity in secondary and tertiary markets. Envious parties immediately begin unbolting, imitating, and redeploying the scraps of cyber-warfare, thus giving birth to a new and growing inventory of cyber-attacks. This vast inventory has been building for years and today we see the commoditization of cyber-attacks – as easy to cart and deliver as anything you might buy on Amazon. In short, the bar for technical skills required to launch attacks is lower than ever, and profits are more easily obtained.

THE UNITED STATES

In 2020, the United States federal government recog- nized an estimated loss of six hundred billion dollars in intellectual property leaking from its government contractors' supply chains.[29] Those government con- tractors, some 300-350,000 entities, all responsible for executing federal contracts, were ill-equipped to handle the data and defenses for our government's classified and unclassified information. If you are curious about how the United States federal govern- ment is responding, just google CMMC 2.0.

THE STATE OF GEORGIA

In 2020, the state of Georgia lost around 700 million dollars due to cyber-attacks.[30] In 2021 losses crested over 1 billion dollars. It is projected that these numbers only represent one-seventh of the actual dollars as so many of the attacks go unreported. If you are curious about how the state of Georgia is responding, just google the Georgia Cyber Crime Center (G3C)

YOUR BUSINESS

The single biggest threat to small businesses today is a cyber-attack. 58% of malware attacks[31] happen to businesses like yours. 60% of small businesses go under within 6 months of a cyber-attack.[32] 80% of businesses that paid a ransom get attacked a second time because the attackers know you'll pay, coupled with the fact that the attackers also know one-in-four businesses don't change or improve their defenses in the wake of a successful attack.[33] If you are curious about how your business is responding, Google won't help, but this chapter will.

Is the wave beginning to have some size and shape for you now? To be clear, I'm still referring to the cyber tsunami wave, which at this point may feel roughly the same size as the wave of anxiety that just washed over your soul. Don't worry, the lifeboat is almost here.

Let's wake up that silent killer thing – not to double down on the anxiety, but to expand the silence. The silence is derived partially from some of the tactical preferences of the attacker. The quieter they are, the less likely you'll notice them sniffing around your office network. If they're quiet, they can take their time to discover where the value is. If they just sit idle in your email communications, for example, you might just tell them when that next wire transfer is about to happen. But the truth is, some attacks are just intended to be loud, disruptive, and malicious. While these attacks are less silent, they are equally as destructive.

The silence also comes in the form of unreported attacks. Unfortunately, some businesses just go out of business. They just can't recover from a cyber-attack and we never hear from them again. The silence can also come indirectly as there can be a level of embarrassment and fear that comes when a business experiences a breach. Owners may not readily know what or how much was compromised. The investigation and forensics could take weeks or months to unravel. Can you just pause everything until that goes away? Who should you tell? What are you obligated to reveal to our clients? What's your liability and financial impact? What will clients think about your ability to conduct business? Will they trust you with their data after this? What about your reputation?

Is this the first time you've thought about this?

Now that we see the numbers, and understand the challenges in front of us, let's talk execution. I realize that if I simply explained the problem and told you WHY a plan was important, this chapter would be as ineffective as your third COVID booster, you'd still have anxiety, and this book would end up under some uneven, but no-longer-wobbling desk leg.

The numbers may be overwhelming, but the path forward does not have to be. Here's the deliverable, the lifeboat:

THE 3-STEP CYBERSECURITY PLAN

Step 1 - Schedule a Cyber Security Risk Assessment

- You can't change what you can't measure. You can't manage risk for data you don't know you have. Get your baseline. Contact a local IT firm, one like PC Techware, that specializes in cyber-security and risk management. This is an assessment that measures risk and vulnerability in your network, data, and devices. The assess-ment should be comprehensive and include dark web scans as well as alerts for your SaaS products. If the assessment can measure your staff's cyber awareness through simulated phishing emails, this can provide valuable insight into the atten-tion/investment you may need to spend on employee training. This assessment should be delivered and presented back to your organiza-tion by the assessor before you make any commitments or decisions about the next steps.

Step 2 – Develop the Plan

- Equipped with the feedback and knowledge you discovered during your Cyber Security Risk

Assessment: you now have a snapshot of your business. In essence, this can become an RFP (Request for Proposal) your business can use to recruit an appropriate I.T. provider for your needs. Or, if you chose an I.T. company to perform your assessment, they are most likely prepared to design a plan that fits your company's needs. So, keep this in mind as you may want to have a qualifying call with several options in your area about their process with clients BEFORE you engage them for Step 1 – the Cyber Security Risk Assessment.

- Pitfall: Without leading them, if a prospective IT company does not suggest a risk assessment as their first step with you as their client, or they can provide you with a proposal of services after a quick walk-through of your organization, you are talking to the wrong partner. Find someone else unless you want to be part of the statistics above.

Step 3 – Execute the Plan

- Plans can vary widely based on an organization's needs, locations, and regulatory or compliance requirements, and a good partner will design a plan specifically for your organization. You may see some combination of hardware/ infrastructure costs, onboarding fees, licensing, cyber-security, monitoring, and management fees. Be sure to understand what sorts of activities, projects, and requests generate an invoice and what does not.

- Prepare for a contracted recurring fee schedule. Protecting your data and reducing your business's risk is never a one-and-done effort. There's no set-it-and-forget-it with IT and cybersecurity. Your technology expense takes constant monitoring and proactive maintenance to ensure things stay tuned and cohesive.

- Get your people trained. There are some fantastic technologies protecting businesses today. There are also fantastic ways to train your employees to become more effective in recognizing attacks and phishing emails. We have a very skilled labor force capable of locking systems down and stopping attacks dead in their tracks. However, if your staff is not properly trained, they can override and enable a cyber-attack out of innocent ignorance. It takes only one email, just one click.

- Transparency: There are several other categories of information you should have as part of your plan. This chapter is intended to guide and inspire, not to serve as a table of contents for your business's plan. Other topics like Data Assurance (Encryption, Offline Backup, and Restoration policies) and Cyber Liability Insurance should be included for example. You should approach your plan with a mindset that allows for maturity over time. Otherwise, you'll get overwhelmed and do nothing.

We have no idea what is still to come. This is not about building the perfect trap inside your business. There is no golden bat for sale. There are no shortcuts. This is old-school pick up the phone, work towards your Cyber

Security Risk Assessment, push for a plan, and then execute. You have the data you need and the 3-Step Plan to make it happen. Keep it small and simple so you can manage it over time.

This chapter is written with the spirit to help you fundamentally elevate your business over time to ensure its survivability against the cyber tsunami. Cybersecurity and IT have evolved so much within the last 5 years that it demands enlisting the help of experts to manage those parts of your business outside your direct area of expertise. The reality is that you cannot be an expert in your field and ours. Your business, your employees, and your clients rely on you staying at the helm and leading the way in your industry. PC Techware is proud to support clients who are experts in the financial, legal, healthcare, construction, manufacturing, and retail verticals. If we can't help you, we will locate an expert in your area who can.

About the Author

Matthew Jay is the Chief Operating Officer at PC Techware, Inc., a systems integration company specializing in Cybersecurity and Risk Management. Some may think 5 years in an industry isn't enough to have stakes in a book like this. But, in an industry that is experiencing a drastic transformation driven by cybercrime that's grown 10 to 12 times within a 12-month period, 5 years is enough time for some products to see their birth and obsolescence. Matthew is no stranger to harnessing disruptive technologies and understands the importance of driving forward to anticipate new problems instead of admiring what's in the rearview mirror.

Matthew enjoys sharing his insights on today's cyber threat landscape with small business owners, professional groups, and local chamber members to create a smarter and more aware workforce. His expertise is rounded out by a close network of family and friends operating in similar technology firms that support small businesses all the way up to the United States Army and Navy.

Matthew has been the humble recipient of a few professional mentors over the course of his career, who have contributed to his leadership skillset, deep experience in lean manufacturing operations, business development of an e-commerce platform, and technology sales within a $22 billion international corporation. In turn, Matthew is passionate about mentoring high school and college students by giving them insight and inspiration as they transition from bookbags to briefcases.

Contact Matthew Jay at:

Website: www.pctechware.com

Email: matt@pctechware.com

Phone: 706-389-0580

LinkedIn: www.linkedin.com/in/matthewjay

How Your Small Business Can Avoid a Data Breach

By Larry Reger

Did you know that almost every business is at risk of experiencing a data breach regardless of its size? Contrary to the belief that they are too small to be targeted, small businesses are commonly victims of cyber-attacks. Cybercriminals are not always looking for the biggest score; they are simply seeking the path of least resistance. Bad actors are trying to get access to any type of sensitive, confidential, or protected data that they can. This may involve personal health information (PHI), personally identifiable information (PII) such as Social Security numbers, driver's license information, and credit card numbers. That path is often opened by small businesses that do not believe they are a target and do not take the proper safety measures. Small business owners should make data security part of the regular routine, like securing their doors at night. Here are a few essential strategies on how your small business can avoid a data breach.

Updates

Operating Systems manage all of the functionality on a computer, so it becomes a primary target for cyber-criminals. Operating Systems do have many built-in functions to help prevent attacks. The issue is that cyber-attacks are constantly changing. This is why operating system vendors regularly offer system updates to keep up with the changing threats from cyber criminals. If the company fails to update its Operating Systems, vulnerabilities occur. In 2017, the WannaCry ransomware attack affected thousands of computers worldwide costing businesses millions of dollars in damages. Yet the exploit used in the attack was patched by Microsoft months before the attack took place. If the affected systems had been properly updated, they would have never been comprised. In a study, BitSight researchers found that of 35,000 companies they studied, more than 50 percent of them were running old or out-of-date browsers (Chrome, Firefox, Edge) making them more than twice as likely to experience a data breach. A compromised web browser could make personal information public and may facilitate the download of spyware that can capture passwords. All software used daily on workstations must be kept up-to-date with the latest versions. Conducting routine updates of all business devices and key software will ensure that you have the latest defenses.

Security Awareness Training

There is not a person alive who has never made a mistake. Making mistakes is a core part of the human experience. It's how we learn and grow. One of the biggest weaknesses in any cybersecurity system is the human factor; this will always be an issue in keeping businesses safe. If employees are not effectively trained on cybersecurity awareness, the chances are very high that they could unknowingly allow a data breach to the business with simple mistakes or apathy. Cybercriminals know this, and they use methods like phishing emails to compromise the entire organization and network. Security Awareness Training is an education program that raises awareness of the various internal and external security risks to a business. It teaches staff about the basics of cybersecurity and how to be more proactive and vigilant. Identifying the right topics that put employees at risk is essential. For example, how to recognize and avoid viruses and malware, how to recognize and avoid phishing and spear phishing scams, secure password use, and social engineering are important. Performing training regularly is important to keep security awareness on the top of the employees' minds, and learning happens through repetition. By doing this, employees will become the greatest asset and not the biggest risk.

Data Protection

Data protection is not just focused on outside threats, businesses need to protect their data from internal threats as well. There is no reason why Jim in marketing would need access to HR data. Implementing the least privilege can help secure access from unauthorized users. This principle enforces a minimal level of user permissions, which allows access to specific files and resources needed to perform a specific job. Restricting user permissions reduces the risk of exploitation in the event the account is compromised. Enabling file auditing is an easy way to track all changes taking place to folders and files. Encrypt all sensitive data. Microsoft BitLocker is a feature that comes with Windows 10 and will encrypt the data on the drive to prevent unauthorized access to your information. Just as it's common practice to keep all sensitive files in a locked cabinet and have a designated gatekeeper who only gives access to those who truly need it, so does the network.

Passwords and Authentication

Implementing strong passwords and authentication is pivotal and should be a minimum baseline for all small businesses. When establishing a password policy, incorporate some of the following best practices: more than 10 characters, at least one upper-case letter, at least one number, and at least 1 special character. Passwords should be hard to guess but easy to remember, changed every few months, and employees should not use the same password for all accounts. Ideally, passwords would be sufficient to authenticate and ensure that users are genuine. Regrettably, passwords are vulnerable to brute force attacks and cyber-criminals are discovering new ways to crack and harvest credentials. Multi-factor Authentication (MFA) is a secure authentication method that requires two or more verification factors to gain access to a resource. This is something you know (username and password), something you have (smartphone or token), and something you are (fingerprint), which decreases the likelihood of a successful cyber-attack. When users log in to online accounts, most web browsers will offer to save the credentials, but these are the first thing cyber-criminals go after when accessing a workstation. Avoid this by implanting password management software. Essentially, it is an encrypted vault for storing passwords that are secured by a master password and a second authentication method. The application can generate long passwords and automatically fill in the credentials for stored sites and synchronize to all devices.

Backup and Recovery

Data breaches are no longer limited to the exposure of confidential data. Ransomware is designed to block access to an organization's data and then demand a ransom to be paid to unlock it. Businesses are placed in a position where paying the ransom is the easiest way to gain access to the files again. However, this is where backing up your data is a key part of the defense against ransomware and securing the network. Unfortunately, many small businesses still do not perform consistent, proper recoverable backups. The ideal backup scenario is to have a combination of on-site, off-site, and cloud backup. This is known as the 3-2-1 approach. Ideally, you would want a solution that runs automatically and provides you with a report if the job completes successfully.

What should you back up? Everything. It's highly recommended that backups be image-based. Since these types of backups are a snapshot of your workstation or server, it can easily be restored to different hardware and be back in business much faster. No matter how the data is backed up, regular test restores need to be conducted to make sure it is recoverable. There is no worse feeling than to find out the backup was not working than after the data is gone. Implementing this backup procedure will give peace of mind to the data's integrity.

BYOD (Bring Your Own Device) Policy

Often, employees use personal devices to work remotely or to connect to the business network. A business's BOYD policy sets out the rules that need to be followed when connecting devices to the network. An example would be clearly defining allowed applications and websites users can access while on the company network. Something to consider if implementing a BYOD policy is a mobile device management solution. This helps centrally manage all mobile devices on the network. This allows for security patching, application management, and updates to be performed on all enrolled mobile devices. When an employee leaves the company, it's important to have the proper procedures in place to ensure any company-sensitive data is removed from the personal device. The policy should include procedures like disabling company emails and changing or removing access to all company accounts. By following these steps and by having a streamlined process to manage devices, the business can reduce the security risk when company employees use personal devices.

End Point Protection

Endpoints (workstations, laptops, mobile devices, and point of sales systems) serve as a point of access to all small businesses that can be exploited by malicious actors. Endpoint security software protects this from risk activity or a malicious attack. With more employees working remotely, it is of the utmost importance that a multilayer approach is taken to protect these devices. A comprehensive endpoint protection measure should include, next-generation antivirus, which can detect malware and other threats even if they do not match known patterns or signatures.

Endpoint detection and response (EDR) provides enhanced visibility and defense measures on the endpoint itself when attacks occur allowing faster response time.

Data Loss Prevention (DLP) software detects potential data breaches / ex-filtration transmissions and prevents them by monitoring and blocking sensitive data while in use, in motion, or at rest. For example, someone is trying to email files to a non-employee, copy files to a flash drive, or upload files to a web-sharing file site.

Application whitelisting is aimed to prevent malicious programs from running on a workstation. It monitors the operating system, in real-time, to prevent any malware from entering and executing within the net-work. It places control on which programs are permitted to run and any program not specifically whitelisted is blocked.

Firewalls also need to be configured to prevent any type of both inbound and outbound. It can stop hackers from attacking your network by blocking specific websites. Laptops and Smartphones also need to be protected with features like data encryption, password protection, MFA, and remote wiping. As cyber threats increase the need for stronger security measures need to be implemented and maintained on all endpoint devices.

With cybercriminals looking for new ways to steal information for their gain, data breaches are becoming more common. It may seem like a tedious or impossible operation to avoid a data breach. There is no silver bullet in cybersecurity. However, with this layered approach to security with various measures, policies, and procedures to mitigate these security threats, your small business will be in a much better state in this ever-changing landscape. To review, some of these multi-layer defenses were:

- Updates

- Security Training

- Data Protection

- Password and Authentication

- Backup and Recovery

- BYOD Policies

- Endpoint Protection

One of the best things to do is establish what the small business's current security posture looks like. How can this be done? Contact an established Managed Services Provider that has a track record of securing and maintaining a well-designed business posture and will perform a Cyber Security Assessment. This assessment will give the business a clear picture of the current state of security and fine-tune IT to reduce the likelihood of a data breach.

About the Author

Larry Reger is an IT & Cybersecurity professional with 20+ years of experience in the IT & Cybersecurity field. Larry is the founder and CEO of LD3 Technology, a managed services provider that helps small & medium businesses in Texas manage their IT and mitigate their risk with Cybersecurity solutions. Larry has earned many certifications throughout his career and has helped LD3 Technology receive and keep multiple industry partnerships with Microsoft and Cisco.

Growing up in South Texas, Larry would go to work with his father and learn to take care of the campus networks. His love for Technology & Networking grew quickly as he continued to spend time with his father building workstations, troubleshooting issues, and learning a deep understanding of all things technology. This led him to a professional degree and a desire to help businesses secure and maintain IT infrastructures. Larry spent the last eleven years developing his business to serve companies as small as 5 users up to over 250 users Statewide. He calls San Antonio, TX home with his wife and three boys.

To schedule a consultation for your business technology needs, please get in touch with us:

Website: http://www.LD3Tech.com

Email: lreger@ld3tech.com

Phone: 210-591-0101

LinkedIn: Larry Reger | LinkedIn

5 Cybersecurity Strategies for Service-Based Businesses

By Claude Louis

One guaranteed way to prevent cybersecurity attacks is to not use technology at all. All you have to do is shift your business back to being cash-based, record all transactions in a ledger, arrive at the doorstep of your vendors to fulfill stock and customer orders, and rely on the phone and the postal service for communications. Easy, right? Of course not. The culture we live in now, especially being in the information age, means using technology in ways to get the most (and hopefully accurate) information, and the best price in the fastest way possible.

As technology leans more toward automation, it is easy to become acclimated to business essentially running itself while we lightly manage the minutiae. Unless you are already running your business off the books, there is zero desire to do so. It's hard to imagine converting any of my businesses into that model. which means if we are going to use technology, we have to have an understanding of where the threats exist within the technology we implement for our businesses.

If you're anything like most business owners, most usually have very little time to understand the fullness of cybersecurity threats or the characteristics of zero-day or zero-hour vulnerabilities and come up with a plan to thwart potential attacks on the business. As a CEO of a 17-year-old technology company and virtual Chief Information Officer (vCIO) for a multitude of companies, I can count on one hand (using no fingers) how many people get excited about discussions of air-gapped computers, man-in-the-middle (MitM) attacks, or Browser in the Browser (BitB) threats.

As fellow business owners, we can relate to the multitude of responsibilities. You must equally protect your business and how it operates in the same regard as your customers and their data. Ultimately, you are held responsible for knowing where the threats to your business exist. And, frankly, we don't know what we don't know. Following a recipe doesn't make you a chef, but you certainly will not starve. Likewise, implementing this recipe of recommendations will not make you a cybersecurity expert, but will it definitely add layers to protect your business interests and cover your ASSets.

Prioritize Cybersecurity

The perpetual evolution of cybersecurity is a lot to keep up with. It seems that for every technological advance made to enhance and protect our trust in technology, some countermeasure is created. You can expect normalcy in the frequency of cyber-attacks reported as you listen to or watch your favorite news source. Let's face it: cybersecurity isn't exactly the hot topic of any dinner conversation or any conversation for that matter. But it is something that, if left unchecked, could devastate the future of your business, or your reputation, and may even earn you some legal liability.

As CEO of Dot Calm in Baton Rouge, Louisiana, we assist clients who are brand new to business and those clients who are already established and need to discuss the proper growth and expansion of their company. We are available nationwide to consult with decision makers by visiting https://dotcalm.it/book to calendar an assessment of your current technology infrastructure.

Identify current systems and processes

Thinking about how many ways our service-based businesses touch the internet can be overwhelming. What's worse is not knowing the function or responsibility of each component and its contingencies. It is obvious to count the computers. But there are a number of other factors to consider like phone systems, surveillance, credit card terminals, website hosting, and backups, just to name a few. Who has passwords to what? What do you do when there is an outage or natural data loss? Do you have a documented means of how technology plays a role in the daily functions of your business?

There is no accurate way to determine the pain points or insufficiencies in your business based on the technology it uses without an accurate "map" of what hardware or software exists, what it is responsible for, and having a regular means of checks and balances to ensure operations are within an acceptable threshold.

Be sure to know what types of technology belong (and what don't) within your organization. Some businesses may consider their size or revenue as a qualifier for outsourcing IT support. However, a proper consultant would be considered wise counsel and it would be strongly encouraged for you to enlist the help of someone to help do the necessary work of identifying processes and how the technology you implement executes those processes. That assistance can be seasonal or ongoing.

In other words, think of it like gardening. You may find it more effective to get the help necessary to break up the soil, pull the weeds, add fertilizer, etc. Once what we would consider the "hard part" is complete, maintaining that garden comes with more ease and is far more manageable.

Update hardware and software regularly

An excellent way to succeed and create a strategy for updating your technology is to first budget for it. While there is no set timeframe to replace your aging technology, a generally accepted consensus is to do so every three years. Some companies do this as often as every 6 months or really stretch the lifespan to 5 years. The bottom line is that you will need to implement a refresh of your hardware on a schedule that makes sense for your business and your budget. Having newer hardware does not just boost performance in the work environment, but it also boasts a heightened security stance. Once you refresh your legacy equipment, be sure to find a means to e-recycle the old hardware in an effort to reduce our carbon footprint.

Software updates should be done as frequently as they are made available, in most cases. As it pertains to the category of upgrading software, it would be awesome if all we needed to do was check for and apply Windows updates. But realistically, there are other aspects of the software to incorporate into your update schedule as well. Examples would be the BIOS for your PCs and firmware for both network and printer equipment.

If you have a website for your business, you should regularly check for updates to the platform and its plugins (if applicable). Remember: when in doubt, ask for QUALIFIED help! As a former firefighter, I found a fitting example that I like to use with many of my clients in knowing when to ask for help. You can ask for help when you smell smoke or you can ask as the entire building is on fire or any of the varying degrees between the two. Ultimately, as in most cases, the sooner a problem is identified, the easier it is to fix.

Here is a Pro tip for my Business Owners: Delete the mindset that your technology spending is an expense. Instead, insert the mindset that your technology spending is an investment.

Educate and Empower Employees

An additional layer to protecting your business as it engages with the world wide web is to educate the people whom you entrust to work within the business.

For starters, this is probably the point where the sticky note with the Wi-Fi password needs to be removed from the edge of the monitor at the front desk. There is a seemingly thinning line between convenience and laziness, but that should never be made to compromise the security of your network or information. Establishing and maintaining the standard for how information is received, stored, and communicated is critical to most organizations and educating employees shares equal importance.

As the nature of business continues to evolve (i.e. work from home), the techniques for maintaining the integrity of the aforementioned information must also evolve. Passwords need complexity and rotation. Two Factor Authentication is a very valuable best practice. Phishing simulations are an example of testing the knowledge of employees.

As October is Cybersecurity Awareness month, make it a mental reminder to encourage awareness. And don't forget to make it fun! While it can be challenging to modify the mindsets of creatures of habit, there are creative ways to make the information relevant and lasting. The National Institute of Standards and Technology, or NIST, has a website with a wealth of resources that will help you to create a system of educating your staff on how to protect themselves. You can visit them online at https://www.nist.gov.

Get Cyber Insurance

If you drive a vehicle, you should have auto insurance. If you are a homeowner, you should have homeowner's insurance. Likewise, if you own a business, you should have business insurance. All are designed to protect your interests in the event of a loss. However, cyber-security incidents are not covered by general liability policies. Nor are they covered by an errors and omissions policy. While an errors and omissions policy would cover events like lawsuits from any misstep between your business and the client, cyber insurance is to help with breaches that affect your business or its data.

Due diligence is recommended in finding a reputable cyber insurance company to assist in minimizing your liability. The application process can be a relatively daunting task and seem rather off-putting. But consid-ering the exposure to the risk of loss and the potential detriment to business and reputation, it is easier to put a proper cyber policy in place now versus trying to figure out an action plan after being hacked, phished out of information, and that information being held at ransom with no guarantee. It is no wonder why 6 out of 10 businesses close within 6 months of being hacked.[34]

Source: https://cybersecurityventures.com/60-percent-of-small-companies-close-within-6-months-of-being-hacked

The above recommendations are simple, yet effective ways to boost your security. While this list is not an end-all-be-all, it is a feasible means of doing something to protect your business instead of doing nothing sleeping on a bed of rabbit's feet or four-leaf clovers. Also, make it a point to calendar regular reminders for reviewing and updating your policies and procedures surrounding cybersecurity as you deem necessary for your business, or better, be sure it is included in your Quarterly Business Reviews with your IT. If you prefer the do-it-yourself route, a great resource to consider is the Cyberplanner provided by the FCC, which can be accessed at https://fcc.gov/cyberplanner. On the website, you can choose topics that are relevant and specific to your business as you implement a strategy to strengthen the cybersecurity of your business.

Some action items can very well be addressed in-house while other tasks will need to be outsourced to qualified talent if you don't have dedicated IT personnel. Nothing against cousins, nephews, or in-laws, but the keyword here is QUALIFIED. A qualified subject matter expert (SME) should not only advise on and implement strategies to reduce the risk of a cyber-attack and the vulnerabilities your business may face, but also have a plan in place to mitigate any cyber-attacks, data loss, or breaches. This person or persons would know what responsibilities and regulations apply to your business as it pertains to who and when to report breaches, depending on the State in which you operate your service-based business.

About the Author

For over two decades, C. Claude Louis, Sr. has been in the technology industry, initially focusing efforts on break-fix services and evolving over time into managed services, VoIP services, web design, and consulting. The name of his company, **Dot Calm**, assists small and medium businesses from across the country in how to use technology to reach their business goals by minimizing downtime and maximizing productivity. As CEO, Claude employs principles of servant leadership, believing firmly in the impact of empowering and developing people. He embodies the philosophy of work not feeling like work when one is passionate about the work.

His love for technology blended with the desire to help others has proved a mutually beneficial working relationship between **Dot Calm** and the over 6,000+ clients they have had the pleasure to work with. After receiving a number of certifications from CompTIA, Dell, and HP, Claude has spent the last 10 years utilizing his knowledge and experience to help develop and grow aspiring technicians new to the industry who need both exposure and experience. Between his work ethic and natural disposition to want to help others, Claude would be the first to tell you that service is in his DNA. This has been displayed not only in his current business operations, but also in his former position as a Firefighter and Emergency Medical Technician for the Baton Rouge Fire Department, where he received certifications, commendations, and life-changing experiences after nearly a decade of service.

When Claude isn't saving the world one computer or network at a time, he is passionate about spending time with two children, Cesare and Lyric. He also can often be found on a pair of roller skates or rollerblades in a host of venues across the country. He enjoys cooking (and especially eating, of course) as well as traveling. Claude also manages a real estate portfolio and aspires to obtain a commercial pilot's license. Claude currently resides in Baton Rouge, Louisiana.

Contact Claude Louis at:

Website: https://www.dotcalm.it

Email: support@dotcalm.it

Phone: (225) 279-2244

Key Cybersecurity Issues Facing the Manufacturing Industry in Today's World

By Dan Di Fulvio

Cybercrime neither has any boundaries nor restricts itself to a specific industry. The manufacturing industry is as vulnerable to cyber-attacks as the finance, healthcare, information technology, or insurance sector. This chapter discusses the cybersecurity issues facing the modern manufacturing industry and how to respond to these threats to ensure the highest safety and security of your critical information assets.

Statistics worldwide show that cybersecurity is among the most significant concern for every industry. A general notion among people is that malicious actors' prime intention is to target network systems only for monetary purposes. However, it is not the case. While money is crucial, a manufacturing organization has much more critical things to lose, such as information assets, known in local parlance as data.[35] Data has tremendous value on the dark web.

Hence, you find adversaries concentrating more on breaching data rather than money. This fact puts all industries, including the manufacturing industry, at risk from cyber-attacks. In this chapter, you will learn how cybersecurity issues can affect the manufacturing industry and what steps one should take to mitigate the risks and ensure the confidentiality, integrity, and availability of critical information assets.

Case Study

Organetix is a multinational medical research and drug manufacturing establishment with patented treatments for Hepatitis. The organization specializes in medical research and drug manufacturing medical devices and products. The manufacturer is leading the way businesses operate and innovate in the global medical device manufacturing industry and continues to be a key player in the world's medical supply chain. The clientele includes some national healthcare service providers, private clinics, and laboratories across the globe. Recently, the organization has been in the news worldwide for all the wrong reasons.

The Problem

The problem started when the first incident of a minor theft of a device surfaced. The petty theft became a significant security incident soon. The investigations revealed that one of the employees was involved in stealing the PII (Personally Identifiable Information) of some of the politicians and HNI (High-Net-worth Individuals) that was stored on an unencrypted device and was allegedly attempting to sell it on the dark web.

Even before the organization could recover from the incident and perform damage control, another incident got reported. The information systems used to process the patient data were compromised by ransomware.

Unfortunately, some of the data was lost during the recovery process as no backup mechanism was in place in the impacted clinic.

The breach resulted in the loss of confidentiality, integrity, and availability of critical and sensitive information. However, the biggest problem that the Organetix management faced was that they never had a comprehensive cybersecurity program to address such issues.

The Solution

The organization immediately mobilized all the resources at its disposal before it was too late. The management called for a meeting of all department heads to discuss the cybersecurity issues and formulate a strategy to deal with them. Addressing the damage that had already occurred was one area of concern. A more concerning issue was preventing a recurrence of the events. Therefore, it called for a multi-pronged approach toward cybersecurity involving every department.

Here is what Organetix decided to be the course of action to mitigate such risks and prevent future cyber misadventures. They chose to use a combination of tactical and strategic moves to deal with the current and future cybersecurity incident(s) if in case it occurs again:

Tactical Plans:

Tactical planning comprehensively outlines the short-term steps the organization can take to overcome a given situation. Organetix was quick in responding to the attacks by:

1. ***Reporting the incident to regulators and communicating it to customers, clients, third-party contractors, and other stakeholders -*** Regulatory compliance is critical because it helps the entire industry to become aware of such cybersecurity issues. In addition, the manufacturer showed its commitment to resolving the issue by sharing the information with its customers, clients, and all stakeholders.

2. ***Investigation and Incident handling-*** The organization ordered an inquiry into the incident and set up an investigation team to probe the issue from all angles. They focused on insider threats first and learned that an employee serving his notice period with the company was involved in data leakage. Besides, the company also fixed a few other loopholes that needed plugging.

3. ***Advising on patching the old operating system*** - Ransomware can infiltrate a network through systems with inadequate security. Therefore, fixing the old operating system and other pieces of software was paramount; an upgrade to a better and more secure OS was advised.

Strategic Plans:

Strategic planning entails establishing goals that can help the organization attain a robust cybersecurity posture for the long term. Organetix decided to use a mix of detective and preventive control measures as part of their strategic planning efforts:

1. ***Setting up a committee to formulate cybersecurity strategies for the future*** - While plugging the holes is a reactive step, the manufacturer decided to go for a proactive approach and set up a committee of experts from all departments to formulate cybersecurity strategies for the future.

2. ***Establishing a comprehensive cybersecurity program to enhance preparedness levels*** - The organization displayed a "Once-bitten-twice-shy" approach by setting up a robust cybersecurity awareness program educating staff members on the threats and risks of cyber-attacks. The program also concentrates on identifying an impending cyber-attack and taking the necessary steps to mitigate the risk.

3. ***Investing in new software and hardware*** - While patching old software is crucial, the organization needs to invest in advanced machines and software that can help them deal with the latest threats.

4. ***Appointing a CISO and providing complete freedom to formulate the requisite cyber-security measures*** - The manufacturer could allocate a fixed security budget and spend money on hiring a full-fledged CISO (Chief Information Security Officer) and give absolute freedom for choosing a solid cybersecurity team to handle potential future threats.

5. ***A people, process, technology-focused approach:*** The way these three elements interact to achieve the enterprise objective can leave gaps or vulnerabilities in the overall system or organizations that adversaries can exploit for their nefarious purposes. The company involved experts in addressing each aspect of people, process, and technology in a way that can enhance collaboration, remove dependencies and SPOF (single point of failures), and proactively detect and respond to any threats.

The Objective

Thus, based on the lessons learned, the chapter will focus on the following aspects:

1. ***Statistics: How Vulnerable the Manufacturing Industry is to Cyber Risks*** - Generally, the manufacturing industry does not involve significant financial transactions. However, they have considerable information that malicious actors can use to extort millions of dollars.

2. **The critical cybersecurity issues facing the manufacturing industry** - Besides the regular phishing, malware, and ransomware attacks, the manufacturing industry is vulnerable to certain specific cybersecurity risks like supply chain attacks, insider threats, IP (Intellectual property) theft, equipment sabotage, IoT (Internet of Things)-based compromise, and even state-sponsored attacks.

3. **Effectively managing cybersecurity issues and risks** - Managing cybersecurity issues involves adopting solutions like SIEM, SOAR, and central-ized intelligence, providing crowdsourced immu-nization for cyber-attacks that the industry has not yet encountered. The following sections examine each of these issues in detail.

Statistics: How Vulnerable the Manufacturing Industry is to Cyber Risks

The following statistics from the last few years display eye-opening information concerning various aspects of cybersecurity threats and attacks, which are as highly pertinent to the manufacturing industry as any other sector.

- A Kaspersky Labs Report states that 77% of industrial organizations rank cybersecurity as the most significant priority. (Kaspersky Labs, 2018).[36]

- The IBM 2022 Report[37] details that the most ransomware-infected industry in 2021 was the manufacturing sector, at 23%. It has overtaken the financial services and the insurance sectors, which used to be the preferred targets of malicious actors. (IBM Report 2022)

- The same IBM Report indicates a 33% increase in attacks because of vulnerability exploitation of unpatched software. Generally, ransomware actors use this vulnerability to launch attacks (IBM Report 2022).

- Gartner predicts that 45% of organizations globally will have experienced cyber-attacks on their software supply chain by 2025. (Gartner Report, 2022)[38]

- The IBM Report 2022 shows malicious actors targeting the cloud environment with a 146% increase in the new Linux ransomware code and a noticeable shift to Docker-focused targeting. (IBM Report, 2022)[39]

The Key Cybersecurity Issues Facing the Manufacturing Industry

Since the manufacturing industry does not frequently deal in large financial transactions, there is a notion that they are immune to cybersecurity risks. However, it forgets that it deals with a more valuable resource, information assets. Malicious actors know that the manufacturing industry does not employ strict security protocols like financial organizations. Hence, they target them for data that can fetch them millions of dollars. Here are some crucial cybersecurity issues facing the manufacturing industry.

Ransomware Attacks

In ransomware attacks, threat actors use a malicious piece of software to encrypt the victim's data. Then, they demand a ransom to decrypt this data, failing which they threaten to leak it or, worse, sell it on the dark web to the highest bidders.

A report from Statista on the industries most affected by ransomware last year placed the manufacturing industry at number 6.[40] It had 22 publicized ransomware attacks, while the government sector was at the top of the list with a score of 47. The accompanying graph shows that every industrial sector is vulnerable to cyber threats. Though the manufacturing industry is in the sixth position, recent trends show that the situation is exacerbating by the day. The IBM 2022 Report clearly states that the manufacturing industry has overtaken industrial sectors like finance and insurance by becoming the prime target for ransomware attacks.

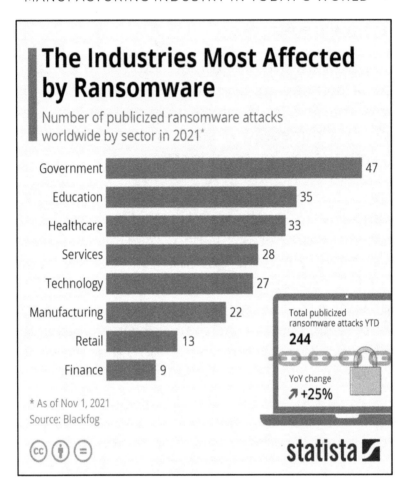

(Image Source: Statista.com)[41]

The data from SonicWall Threat Report 2022 points to an increase of 105% in ransomware attacks due to the pandemic's unprecedented growth in remote and hybrid work.[42] This available data is only the tip of the iceberg as you have various organizations not reporting ransomware attacks but silently paying off the ransom.

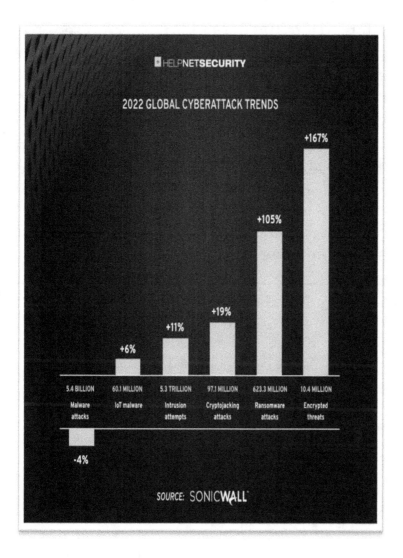

(Source: Help Net Security*)⁴³*

Social Engineering and Phishing Attacks

According to Zscaler's 2022 ThreatLabz Phishing Report, manufacturing was the second most targeted industry by phishing attacks, after retail/wholesale. Phishing involves using social engineering tactics by threat actors to lure the target into divulging sensitive or confidential information, which can then be used for various malicious purposes, including but not limited to corporate espionage, identity thefts, and launching other cyber-attacks. With more people on the internet than ever at any given time, especially smartphone WiFi, adversaries have a wider net to spread and look out for victims. The concepts of IoT and shared net-works make it even more alarming because all an infiltrator needs is to compromise one vulnerable device to access the entire network.

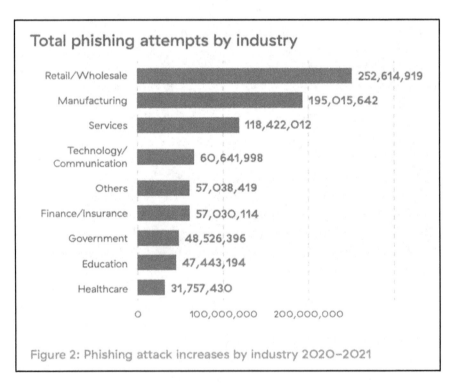

Total phishing attempts by industry

Retail/Wholesale	252,614,919
Manufacturing	195,015,642
Services	118,422,012
Technology/Communication	60,641,998
Others	57,038,419
Finance/Insurance	57,030,114
Government	48,526,396
Education	47,443,194
Healthcare	31,757,430

Figure 2: Phishing attack increases by industry 2020–2021

(Source: Zscaler)[44]

Insider Threats

It may lead to the theft of IP (Intellectual Property), sensitive and confidential financial data, business secrets, etc. Insider threats are the most wicked because they erode the fundamental values of trust that the industry has in its employees. IBM's Annual Insider Threat Report indicates that employee or contractor negligence accounted for nearly 63% of insider threats.[45]

Supply Chain Attacks

In these attacks, cybercriminals target the weakest link in the supply chain. As manufacturing organizations have to stay connected with multiple third-party entities, they become highly vulnerable to supply chain attacks; although the manufacturing organization itself may have a robust cybersecurity posture, an outside vendor it deals with may not be following the best cybersecurity practices. An ENISA Report says that supply chain attacks are on the rise, affecting the manufacturing industry more than anything else.[46] While 66% of the episodes focus on the supplier's code, 62% exploit the trust between the customers and the supplier. The report further states that 58% of the attacks concentrate on accessing data, with 62% relying on malware.

Equipment Sabotage

Equipment sabotage attacks involve damaging or obstructing the working of machinery involved in various manufacturing processes by infiltrating the software that controls it. One recent equipment sabotage attack in the medical equipment manufacturing industry involved compromising Stradis Healthcare's shipping system, where the perpetrators disrupted the delivery of personal protective equipment kits in the middle of the global pandemic. (McGee M K, 2020)[47]

Zero-Day Vulnerabilities

Zero-day vulnerabilities are those that the manufacturer has not yet discovered, and thus there is a risk that threat actors could exploit them. With almost every manufacturing activity being computerized today, zero-day vulnerability issues are rising. While the manufacturing industry might not immediately feel the impact of a zero-day vulnerability, one cannot rule out the threat. Besides data theft, it can cause loss to production, reputational loss, watering hole attacks, and legal implications.

Effectively Managing Cybersecurity Issues and Risks

Manufacturing establishments can effectively mitigate cybersecurity risks and thwart threats by following the security best practices listed below.

- ***Building a Robust Cybersecurity Culture:*** Cybersecurity is everyone's responsibility, from C-level executives to junior-level employees. Everyone should understand their responsibilities and do their bit towards managing cybersecurity risks by appropriately handling the information.

- **Following Basic Cyber-Hygiene:** Remembering and following cyber-hygiene best practices that everyone needs to seriously consider while dealing with information to keep the organization cyber-safe. These include using strict passwords, 2FA (2-Factor Authentication), not opening email attachments that came via unknown sources, etc.

- **Cybersecurity Training, Education, and Awareness:** Every industry should concentrate on training its employees and creating awareness of cybersecurity risks. The focus should be on educating employees to identify the risk signals and take appropriate action. Imparting knowledge of reporting any incident is critical because it enables the security team to initiate prompt remedial steps to contain threats.

- **Securing Operations:** Malicious actors keep looking for vulnerabilities in the systems to exploit. Therefore, it becomes imperative for the industry to plug the holes and patch up the software loopholes. Besides, these securing operations should be ongoing, and all the network systems should be equipped with updated anti-malware solutions to enable the industry to remain one step ahead of the malicious actors.

- **Effective Threat Detection:** Detecting cyber threats on time is critical to risk mitigation. Organizations should implement threat detection tools like SIEM (Security Information and Event Management) that provide regular alerts enabling the administrator to take prompt remedial action. Besides SIEM, SOAR (Security Orchestration, Automation, and Response) is crucial because it automates the investigation path and reduces the time required to mitigate the threat. Together SIEM and SOAR can improve the cybersecurity posture of the organization.

- **Effective Threat Prevention:** Detecting threats is one aspect of cybersecurity, whereas prevention by anticipating them is critical. Some effective threat prevention measures include having a well-defined IAM (Identity and Access Management) system with strong passwords, conditional, need-to-know, and least-privilege-based access to systems, etc., to prevent insider threats. In addition, updating the anti-malware solutions is critical to effective threat prevention. Finally, educating and creating awareness among personnel, as mentioned earlier, is equally crucial.

- **Implementing a Comprehensive Cybersecurity Program:** There are no stopgap measures regarding cybersecurity. One loophole is sufficient for malicious cyber actors to access the network and cause irreparable damage. Hence, it is advisable to enforce a comprehensive cybersecurity program that investigates the minutest of details to ensure the highest levels of security.

- **Effective Communication:** While enforcing a high-level cybersecurity program is inevitable for every manufacturing organization, compliance with the security norms is paramount. Reporting to regulatory authorities is a crucial aspect of compliance. Similarly, every organization has a responsibility towards all its stakeholders. Maintaining data privacy is of tremendous significance. Therefore, it becomes essential to communicate effectively with all affected or relevant parties whenever there is a threat of a data breach.

Conclusion

No one can ever ignore cyber threats or sweep them under the carpet. The only way to deal with cyber threats is to have an effective cybersecurity program. Detecting the risks in advance is crucial as it helps minimize damage considerably. However, some threats are inevitable because no manufacturing organization can guarantee that its network systems are 100% immune to cyber threats. Therefore, every manufacturer should have a robust incident response mechanism to help deal with the threats effectively and prevent them from causing financial or reputational losses and harm.

And certain areas in the current manufacturing scenario need special attention. For instance, the Internet of Things, or IoT, is increasingly becoming an indispensable part of modern manufacturing and industrial processes and can be a source of many vulnerabilities. Due to low time-to-market demands, the IoT scene is often fast and dynamic, making such systems highly vulnerable. It warrants that security precautions be embedded in such systems in the design stage itself, a concept known as 'Security by Design' (SbD) for the best security.

About the Author

Dan Di Fulvio is the Founder and CEO of HERO Managed Services, and veteran of providing technology management and support for over 20 years. Dan is the key driving force behind a business dedicated to providing unmatched customer service and technology solutions for SMB clients through the Tampa Bay area. Dan's success stems not only from extensive industry expertise and passion for technology, but from the ability to understand and meet the needs his customers, and to establish long-term relationships based on trust, dedication, and dependability.

HERO is an IT Services and Cloud Computing Provider located in Clearwater Florida focused on providing unmatched customer service and technology solutions for SMB clients through the US. HERO's cost-effective IT solutions are custom designed to deliver our customers a secure and dependable technology environment, 24x7 access to qualified support professionals, highest-quality customer service, and guaranteed piece of mind that they no longer have to worry about IT.

Visit our website at https://www.heromanaged.com and inquire about a cybersecurity assessment or to submit your contact information to have a quick chat about how we can help your business continue to grow.

Contact Dan Di Fulvio at:

Website: https://www.heromanaged.com/

Email: dan@heromanaged.com

Phone: 813-997-6983

LinkedIn: https://www.linkedin.com/in/dandifulvio/

Resources for this chapter

1. Morris, M. (2022, March 30). *2022 trends to look out for in the industrial cybersecurity industry.* Forbes. https://www.forbes.com/sites/forbestechcouncil/2022/03/30/2022-trends-to-look-out-for-in-the-industrial-cybersecurity-industry/?sh=27b3bf6c20f9
2. Manufacturing.net. *The state of manufacturing cybersecurity in 2022.* (2022, February 7). https://www.manufacturing.net/software/blog/22043504/the-state-of-manufacturing-cybersecurity-in-2022
3. Trend Micro. (2022, June 6). Cyber-attacks on industrial assets cost firms millions. https://www.trendmicro.com/en_hk/about/newsroom/press-releases/2022/06-06-2022.html
4. Toth, P. (2022, May 11). *Cybersecurity and Industry 4.0 – what you need to know.* NIST. https://www.nist.gov/blogs/manufacturing-innovation-blog/cybersecurity-and-industry-40-what-you-need-know
5. Dibrov, Y. (2022, February 3). *Cybersecurity in the industry 4.0 era.* Forbes. https://www.forbes.com/sites/forbestechcouncil/2022/02/03/cybersecurity-in-the-industry-40-era/?
6. Deloitte. (2022). *Securing Industry 4.0.* https://www2.deloitte.com/content/dam/Deloitte/be/Documents/risk/securing-industry-4.0-2022_deloitte-be-en.pdf
7. Ic3.gov. (2022, February 11). Indicators of Compromise Associated with BlackByte Ransomware. https://www.ic3.gov/Media/News/2022/220211.pdf
8. CISA. (2022, February 10). *2021 trends show increased globalized threat of ransomware.* https://www.cisa.gov/uscert/ncas/alerts/aa22-040a
9. Miller, J. (2021, July 1). *Top 7 cyber threats for manufacturing companies.* Bitlyft. https://www.bitlyft.com/resources/cyber-threats-manufacturing-companies
10. Avertium. (2022, May 10). *The top 5 cyber threats within the manufacturing industry.* https://www.avertium.com/resources/threat-reports/top-5-threats-within-manufacturing
11. Verizon. (2022). *Data Breach Investigations Report 2008-2022.*
12. https://www.verizon.com/business/resources/reports/2022/dbir/2022-data-breach-investigations-report-dbir.pdf
13. IBM. (2020). *Cost of Insider Threats: Global Report.*
14. https://www.ibm.com/downloads/cas/LQZ4RONE

End Notes

_____

[1] https://www.verizon.com/business/resources/reports/dbir/2022/summary-of-findings/

[2] https://www.privacyaffairs.com/dark-web-price-index-2021/

[3] https://www.ibm.com/downloads/cas/G6E26E3J

[4] https://www.fundera.co/resources/small-business-cyber-security-statistics

[5] https://www.experian.com/blogs/ask-experian/what-is-dark-web-monitoring/

[6] https://www.acronyms.co.uk/blog/backup-rule-of-three/

[7] https://www.makeuseof.com/tag/3-things-antivirus-doesnt-take-care/

[8]https://www.trendmicro.com/vinfo/us/security/definition/managed-detection-and-response

[9] https://expertinsights.com/insights/what-are-email-security-gateways-how-do-they-work-and-what-can-they-offer-your-organization/

[10] https://www.mimecast.com/content/what-is-security-awareness-training/

[11] https://blog.rsisecurity.com/the-importance-of-a-cybersecurity-risk-assessment/

[12] https://www.ibm.com/downloads/cas/OJDVQGRY

[13] https://www.upguard.com/blog/essential-eight

[14] https://www.data3.com/knowledge-centre/blog/essential-eight-maturity-model-user-application-hardening/

[15] https://www.pcmag.com/news/tesla-targeted-in-hack-from-russian-who-tried-to-pay-employee-to-plant.)

[16] https://www.microsoft.com/security/blog/2021/03/02/hafnium-targeting-exchange-servers/

[17] https://learn.microsoft.com/en-us/answers/questions/517533/ pint-server-and-print-nightmare-update.html

[18] https://www.zdnet.com/article/this-is-how-long-hackers-will-spend-in-your-network-before-deploying-ransomware-or-being-spotted/

[19] https://www.cnbc.com/2022/04/14/conti-ransomware-leak-shows-group-operates-like-normal-tech-company.html

[20] https://www.bbc.com/news/business-59990477

[21] https://www.theguardian.com/world/2022/feb/27/anonymous-the-hacker-collective-that-has-declared-cyberwar-on-russia

[22] https://www.theatlantic.com/technology/archive/2020/08/ hacker-group-anonymous-returns/615058/

[23] https://www.forbes.com/sites/thomasbrewster/2019/08/06/att-insiders-bribed-with-over-1-million-to-unlock-2-million-phones-and-hack-their-employer-doj-claims/?sh=7128983ace1e

[24] https://www.justice.gov/opa/pr/fraudster-sentenced-prison-long-running-phone-unlocking-scheme-defrauded-att

[25] https://www.nist.gov/blogs/taking-measure/cybercrime-its-worse-we-thought

[26] https://www.fundera.com/resources/small-business-cyber-security-statistics

[27] https://cybersecurityventures.com/hackerpocalypse-cybercrime-report-2016/

[28] https://cybersecurityventures.com/jobs/

[29] https://www.defense.gov/News/News-Stories/Article/Article/2071434/dod-to-require-cybersecurity-certification-in-some-contract-bids/

[30] https://www.wfxg.com/story/45568960/cyber-news-now-gbi-anticipates-increased-cyber-crime-trend-for-2022

[31] https://www.comparitech.com/blog/information-security/human-error-cybersecurity-stats/

[32] https://www.fundera.com/resources/small-business-cyber-security-statistics

[33] https://www.securityweek.com/it-doesnt-pay-pay-study-finds-eighty-percent-ransomware-victims-attacked-again

[34] https://cybersecurityventures.com/60-percent-of-small-companies-close-within-6-months-of-being-hacked

[35] Huelsman, T. Cyber risk in advanced manufacturing. Deloitte. https://www2.deloitte.com/us/en/pages/manufacturing/articles/cyber-risk-in-advanced-manufacturing.html

[36] Kaspersky. (2018, June) The State of Industrial Cybersecurity 2018. https://ics.kaspersky.com/media/2018-Kaspersky-ICS-Whitepaper.pdf

[37] IBM. (2022, February 23). IBM report: Manufacturing felt brunt of cyberattacks in 2021 as supply chain woes grew. https://newsroom.ibm.com/ 2022-02-23-IBM-Report-Manufacturing-Felt-Brunt-of-Cyberattacks-in-2021-as-Supply-Chain-Woes-Grew

[38] Gartner. (2022, April 13). 7 top trends in cybersecurity for 2022. https://www.gartner.com/en/articles/7-top-trends-in-cybersecurity-for-2022

[39] https://newsroom.ibm.com/2022-02-23-IBM-Report-Manufacturing-Felt-Brunt-of-Cyberattacks-in-2021-as-Supply-Chain-Woes-Grew

[40] https://www.statista.com/chart/26148/number-of-publicized-ransomware-attacks-worldwide-by-sector/

[41] https://www.statista.com/chart/26148/number-of-publicized-ransomware-attacks-worldwide-by-sector/

[42] https://blog.sonicwall.com/en-us/2022/06/cybersecurity-news-trends-6-24-22/

[43] https://www.helpnetsecurity.com/2022/02/18/rise-ransomware-attacks/

[44] Zscaler. (2022). 2022 ThreatLabz Phishing Report. https://www.zscaler.com/resources/industry-reports/2022-threatlabz-phishing-report.pdf?

[45] IBM. (2020). Cost of Insider Threats: Global Report.

https://www.ibm.com/downloads/cas/LQZ4RONE

[46] ENISA. (2021, July 29). *Understanding the increase in Supply Chain Security Attacks.* https://www.enisa.europa.eu/news/enisa-news/understanding-the-increase-in-supply-chain-security-attacks

[47] McGee, M. (2020, April 23). *Prosecutors: Insider "sabotaged" medical equipment shipments.* Bankinfosecurity. https://www.bankinfosecurity.com/prosecutors-insider-sabotaged-medical-equipment-shipments-a-14172

www.ingramcontent.com/pod-product-compliance
Lightning Source LLC
LaVergne TN
LVHW022312060326
832902LV00020B/3426